EMINENT DOMAIN
by Laura Leininger-Campbell

Prairie Moon Publishing, Inc.
301 South 50th Avenue
Omaha NE 68132
eminent@mcwriting.com

Updated May 2025

This is a work of fiction. Names, characters, and incidents either are the product of the author's imagination or are used fictitiously. Any resemblance to real persons, living or dead, is purely coincidental.

Book and cover design: Michael Campbell
Cover photo by Laura Leininger-Campbell

ISBN: 978-1-62660-135-2

Learn more at www.lalaplaywright.com

EMINENT DOMAIN

a play by

Laura Leininger-Campbell

"Laura Leininger-Campbell's *Eminent Domain* exquisitely captures the beating heart of a community, and the fierce loyalty within a family. I am proud and honored to see this story enter the canon of American theatre."

KIMBERLY FAITH HICKMAN, ARTISTIC DIRECTOR
OMAHA COMMUNITY PLAYHOUSE

"With *Eminent Domain,* Laura Leininger-Campbell turned her activism into art. She has given a voice to those directly affected by the proposed Keystone pipeline in a unique, human and important manner. Artists have a responsibility to comment on the events that surround them, and Laura has done that in a truly stunning way."

BETH THOMPSON, ARTISTIC DIRECTOR
SHELTERBELT THEATRE

"Laura has created an important, relevant and moving piece of art in *Eminent Domain;* but more importantly she has intentionally and beautifully captured the dynamics of a Nebraska farm family and the struggles and joys they experience together. The authenticity of her characters makes this piece transcend time, setting and climate."

KATIE BROMAN, EXECUTIVE DIRECTOR
OMAHA COMMUNITY PLAYHOUSE

"Laura's words bring to life the emotional journey Nebraska farmers and ranchers are facing as they struggle to protect their land from eminent domain. The play *Eminent Domain* captures the injustice to what we hold as deep American values — that our land is part of our family heritage. Laura's endless nights writing this story educating Americans about the abuse of eminent domain hopefully means fewer sleepless nights for landowners who go to bed and wake up every day wanting to protect the land."

JANE KLEEB, FOUNDER OF BOLD NEBRASKA AND
CHAIR OF THE NEBRASKA DEMOCRATIC PARTY

CONTENTS

VI

PRODUCTION HISTORY

Eminent Domain saw its world premiere at the Omaha Community Playhouse in Omaha, Nebraska on August 25, 2017 (Katie Broman, Executive Director; Kimberly Faith Hickman, Artistic Director). The production was directed by Amy Lane, with Assistant Director Garett Garniss. Set and lighting design was by Jim Othuse, and costumes were designed by Megan Kuehler. Sound design by John Gibilisco, using original music composed for *Eminent Domain* by Michael Campbell. The Production Stage Manager was Steve Priesman, Darin Kuehler was Properties Designer, and Greg Scheer was the Production Coordinator.

ORIGINAL CAST:

ROB MacLEOD . . . . Bill Hutson

ADAIR MacLEOD. . . . . Erika Hall Sieff

BART MacLEOD . . . . Jeremy Estill

THERESA MacLEOD . . . . Christina Rohling

CAM MacLEOD. . . . . Cork Ramer

JANE MacLEOD. . . . . Judy Radcliff

EVAN MacLEOD . . . . Eric Salonis

TRENT NICHOLS . . . . Chris Shonka

MAT SALINAS. . . . . Thomas Becker

FOREWORD

Living and working in the arts in Nebraska can be a challenge. Especially since our American theatrical landscape is centered in larger cities, we are inundated almost exclusively with stories of New York, Chicago, Los Angeles and the like. It is very rare for me to pick up a script and discover a family I am so familiar with, characters that seem to be drawn from my childhood memories, characters who understand the beauty of a Nebraska landscape and the importance of belonging to the land. From the first lines of *Eminent Domain,* one thought kept resounding in my mind: *This is me. This is us, all of us here who call Nebraska home. This is our story.*

Laura captures the fierce loyalty this family feels to their heritage and understands with the deepest compassion the necessity of protecting their legacy. This has been a beautiful journey bringing this play to life. Thank you, Laura, for telling our story.

Amy Lane,
Assistant Professor of Theatre
Creighton University

Dedicated to my parents,
Steve and Sandy Leininger,
who continue to care for the family land.

CAST OF CHARACTERS

ROB MacLEOD:. . . . . . 60's; a rancher and farmer

ADAIR MacLEOD: . . . . 30's; Rob's daughter, an attorney

BART MacLEOD:. . . . . 30's; Rob's son, a rancher and farmer

THERESA MacLEOD:. . 30's; Bart's wife

CAM MacLEOD: . . . . . 60's; Rob's brother, also a farmer

JANE MacLEOD: . . . . . 60's; Cam's wife

EVAN MacLEOD:. . . . . 30's; Cam and Jane's son, autistic

TRENT NICHOLS:. . . . 40's; an employee of Canadian Energy

MAT SALINAS: . . . . . . 40's; an attorney

PLACE

The MacLeod Family Ranch; Nance County, Nebraska.

TIME

A growing season. Present day.

A NOTE ON THE TEXT:

A line ending in a dash (/) should prompt actors to immediately respond on the following line.

EMINENT DOMAIN

PART ONE

Palm Sunday

*Lights up on the living room of the MacLeod farmhouse. It
is late afternoon/early evening. Spring light shines through
the windows; you can see the fields beyond. The living room
is neat, but noticeably shabby, tired. On the walls and mantle
are family pictures, framed diplomas, documents, deeds, and
Scottish memorabilia associated with the Clan MacLeod. There
is a display on one of the antique tables of a family crest, plaid,
and an ornamental sword. TRENT NICHOLS and ROB
MacLEOD stand, facing each other.*

ROB

You sure you're good with water?

TRENT

Water will be fine.

ROB

Sure you don't want something stronger?

TRENT

No, I'm good.

ROB

(To kitchen) Got a fourteen-year-old scotch back here.

TRENT

Thank you, I'll be fine.

*ROB exits to the kitchen. TRENT is alone in the living room. He
walks around it, looking at the pictures on the mantel, the deeds*

on the wall. He sees the display of Scottish memorabilia, and picks up the sword, awkwardly. ROB enters, with glass of water, a bottle of scotch and two extra glasses. TRENT turns, and finds himself pointing the sword at ROB.

ROB

Maybe I should stay sober for this meeting.

TRENT

(Snaps to attention, puts down the sword quickly) Uh. I was—I'm sorry. I saw a real live sword and just had to pick it up.

ROB

Huh. You know, I got teased a lot for being the runt of the family. Maybe I'm overcompensating for something. What do you think?

TRENT

(After a beat. Pointing at crest) So, your family comes from Scotland?

ROB

Highlands. Isle of Skye. *(He crosses to TRENT, hands him the water.)* Pressure getting to you?

TRENT

Pressure?

ROB

Pressure's dropping. *(Indicates a barometer)* That storm front's coming in. *(He goes to the sofa, sits, pours himself a drink).* How long have you been here now?

TRENT

About six months, Mr. MacLeod.

ROB

Please, call me Rob. I'll tell you, Mr. Nichols. I do love watching a storm come in.

TRENT

Trent, please.

ROB

Feels like every blade of grass reaches up a little higher to watch for it on the horizon.

TRENT

Have you ever seen a twister?

ROB

I've seen many. *(Holds up the bottle)* Single malt this fine is made for telling stories…

TRENT

(Smiles) Twelve years, huh?

ROB

(Grins) You think I'm a heathen? *Fourteen,* Trent.

TRENT

Well, you have me intrigued now.

ROB

(Pours) So. Saw my first twister when I was a kid. It slithered above our field like one of them black snakes the swamis tempt out of the baskets?

TRENT

A cobra?

ROB

That's it! They hypnotize you just the same. Just stood there with my Dad, staring stupid at it until my brother Cam came screaming up the road, pulling on our sleeves to run.

TRENT

Lucky for you your brother was looking out for you.

ROB

(Chuckling) Lucky for me my brother's got the mental constitution of a wet cat. You can tell him I said that.

TRENT

(Laughing) Oh, I don't think I will.

ROB

Okay. Another one? (TRENT nods yes, ROB pours.) Yes sir, I do believe that was the first time I felt the presence and the power of God.

TRENT

Your brother mentioned you memorized entire passages of the Bible as a child.

ROB

Huh. Probably told you I don't go to church anymore these days.

TRENT

He did.

ROB

But. I will tell you this, Trent. I am a God-fearing man.

TRENT

Thank you again for agreeing to meet with me today, Mr. MacLeod.

ROB

Rob. Besides, if I kept saying no to you, Trent, my brother would kick my ass.

TRENT

(Laughs) Oh, I don't know if he would do that...

ROB

Why do you think I keep that sword handy? "A brother is born for adversity." Proverbs 17.

TRENT

I believe it's a sign of strength in a man who knows the word of God by heart.

ROB

It is a truth I've tried real hard to understand His ways.

TRENT

You know, Cam told me a story about how you got your wife to go out with you.

ROB

(*Laughs, pours another round*) Ah, God! Billie was the prettiest girl in Sunday school. (*Winks*) She dared me to read the 'dirty bits' of the Bible in front of the entire congregation: Song of Solomon. And I memorized it and delivered it straight to her: "Daughter of Jerusalem, I charge you: do not arouse or awaken love until it so desires. Place me as a seal on your arm, for love is as strong as death. It burns like blazing fire. Rivers cannot wash it away." (*ROB drinks*)

TRENT

I'm sorry for your loss.

ROB

Thank you.

TRENT

(*Motions to the mantle*) Tell me about your children.

ROB

Well, there's my son Bart and his wife Theresa—

TRENT

I know them from church.

ROB

I wasn't aware.

TRENT

I'm still pretty new to town. I think it takes time for folks to feel more comfortable with…

ROB

Canadians?

TRENT

I'm from Ohio.

ROB

You seem Canadian.

TRENT

No-no, my company's based in Canada, but there's a lot of us here in the states.

ROB

(Measuring him up) Huh.

TRENT

And you have a daughter as well, I'm told?

ROB

Adair. She lives in California.

TRENT

That sounds lovely.

ROB

She's a communist.

TRENT

Oh.

ROB

Whoops. Can't say the words I want to any more. I'm failing in political correct these days.

TRENT

I see.

ROB

God knows there's a verse in the Good Book about the aggravation daughters inflict upon their fathers.

TRENT

I understand she's quite a skillful attorney.

ROB

Now where did you hear that?

TRENT

Your brother's wife, Jane? She told me about all of you. And your wife, of course.

ROB

Well, if it was Jane, I'm sure she painted quite a vivid picture of us all. *(He stands, and goes to the mantel.)* You looking to build a family, Trent?

TRENT

Some day, Rob. God willing. I hope so.

ROB

Hard to raise a family here. Hard to keep 'em home. Have you ever heard of St. Kilda?

TRENT

St. Kilda? No. Who was she?

ROB

(Laughs wistfully) St. Kilda is an island off the coast of Scotland. Billie and I went there. Villages and farmland as beautiful as Brigadoon; and now all the people are gone. All of the youngsters left for a life on the mainland in the 1930's. And in the end, they couldn't sustain. An entire generation vanished inside of a decade. There were only 36 people remaining on St. Kilda. So the Scottish

government made them an offer. A very hard compromise. The elders could all evacuate to the mainland forever, but no animal or human could remain. Nothing there now but crumbling foundations.

Distant lightning and faint thunder. ROB stares out the window.

ROB

You're here to offer me something, aren't you.

TRENT

Yes sir.

ROB

Okay. Let's see it.

TRENT reaches into a briefcase, and pulls out a sheaf of documents—maps, assessor documentation, contracts. As he places them on the coffee table, ROB refills their glasses.

TRENT

All right. We are requesting an agreement with you to sell an easement to Canadian Energy Corporation, on this northeast section of your farm. This easement will allow us to bury a pipeline containing tarsands oil originating in our oil fields in Alberta, and terminating near Galveston bay. *(He points)* Point of entry on your land will begin here, continuing southwest, meeting your brother Cam's pasture. *(He leans forward and smiles at ROB)* Now, here's why I'm excited to talk with you today: We know this farm is your legacy. And my company is aware that you have had… *reservations* considering our proposal. *(He pushes a piece of paper across the table to ROB)* As such, here is a significant increase in this offer. *Your* offer. We know that this decision has weighed heavily on you, and we hope this offer underscores our commitment in this new partnership.

ROB picks up the paper and reads.

ROB

This underscore of yours has a lot of zeroes.

TRENT

Yes.

ROB

How far deep will this pipeline go?

TRENT

Four feet. Deep enough for you to plow and harvest. You'll never know we're here.

ROB

And what do your scientists say about the alkali content in my ground soil?

TRENT

(Reaches for a document) That's a great question, Rob. Now, our analysis shows the alkali content in your land is a sandy grade, and it *is* of a higher percentage; however, you'll see that in tests of the chemical sealant we use, it will withstand that level very well.

ROB

How long?

TRENT

To withstand?

ROB

Trent, I change out my fenceposts because the sand and the salt in my land eats through them like they're made out of cheese. Your pipeline will be underground a lot longer.

TRENT

I trust our scientists. We have the best chemists—

ROB

In Canada.

TRENT

(*Chuckles*) America too. We spare no expense to make sure that the pipeline is safe.

ROB

And if it breaks?

TRENT

It won't.

ROB

Never?

TRENT

No.

ROB

Pinky swear?

TRENT

God forbid, if there were to be some kind of breach, then Canadian Energy would own and lead any cleanup.

ROB

If you caused it.

TRENT

Swear to God.

> *Thunder rolls louder in the distance. Trent holds out his hand. ROB considers, then decides to shake.*

ROB

(*Grins*) Lot of zeroes.

TRENT

(*Grins back*) Yes, Rob. Lot of zeroes.

ROB

Got a pen?

TRENT pulls a pen from his jacket, hands it to ROB, who takes it, and leans over the document to sign. TRENT takes a long pull on his drink.

ROB

Sorry. One more question.

TRENT

Yes?

ROB

(Squinting) What's all this language here? Is this Canadian? *(Both men laugh)*

TRENT

No, this is Latin. Lawyers love their Latin. "The party of the first part," et cetera…

ROB

(Looks back down at the document) I'm looking at the section here about liability. There's a couple of words in here: *"casus fortuitus."* What does that mean?

TRENT

"Casus fortuitus?" *(Thinks)* Huh. Ah, I don't know offhand. But after we're done here, I can give the office / a call

ROB

If I read this paragraph correctly, it sounds like Canadian Energy would be liable for any damages to my land caused by the pipeline, *except* for this *"casus fortuitus."* Does that sound right to you?

TRENT

(Carefully) That feels accurate. I wish I understood Latin.

ROB

Ficta voluptatis causa sint proxima veris.

TRENT

   (After a beat) What?

ROB

   "In order to please, fictions should approximate the truth." I took Latin in college.

TRENT

   Oh.

ROB

   (Wolfish smile) Pretty good at it too. So, let's go back to this phrase here, Trent: *"casus fortuitus."* I'm pretty sure that means "chance occurrence." Or, another phrase that you see a lot in contracts: *"force majeure."*

TRENT

   (Snaps his fingers) Oh yes! "Act of God."

ROB

   (Snaps his fingers) Act of God.

     Lightning flashes simultaneously with a loud thunderclap.

TRENT

   (Quickly) Well, I know what that means. That just means if there's a tornado, or a hurricane.

ROB

   No hurricanes here.

TRENT

   But the pipeline will be buried so deeply underground, a tornado wouldn't damage it.

ROB

   And what about the soil, Trent?

TRENT

The soil?

ROB

The alkali content. Let's say over time, the sand and salt *does* grind through the pipeline enough that it bleeds all your Canadian grease down into the aquifer. Time and decay sounds an *awful* lot like something in God's wheelhouse. Would you call *that* an act of God, Trent?

TRENT

You know, I'm not really sure, Rob.

ROB

Call me Mr. MacLeod.

TRENT

That scenario is something that I would need to take / back to

ROB

(*Interrupting*) To all your scientists and engineers and goddamn lawyers.

TRENT

Excuse me. The odds of a leak are so minuscule/ that it's not

ROB

Oh, give me a break. I'm not a fool.

TRENT

I'm not saying you are.

ROB

You are if you expect me to accept those odds! Anyone would be a fool or an idiot to bet money against a fucking act of God!

TRENT

I'm not sure I appreciate your language, sir. I thought you told me you were a God-fearing man!

ROB

Oh, I *am* a God-fearing man. I fear the fuck out of Him.

TRENT

(TRENT stands up a little too quickly, stumbles a little.) What did you say??

ROB

(Grinning, wild-eyed) However! I never said I *respected* him! Fuck that guy. *(Lightning and thunder crashes. TRENT jumps at the sound. ROB points and laughs)* AHHAHAHA! Right there! You see that??? That dickhead has my number!!!

TRENT

Oh my God.

ROB

Well, thanks for stopping by! *(Takes the papers)* You have a good day now!

TRENT passes ROB on the way to the door. He stops.

TRENT

Mr. MacLeod! You are squandering a chance to protect your family's future.

ROB

(Shooing him out the door) Their future will never be tied to you or your / company, Mr. Nichols.

TRENT

Excuse me! You don't understand how my company works, Mr. MacLeod. We have resources and we have patience. You say your God loves time and decay? So do we. We *will* establish a lawful transaction of this easement, whether or not you agree. We don't care.

ROB

What did you just say to me?

TRENT

I said we don't care! We *will* file a claim of eminent domain against you in order to complete this pipeline. We're here and we're staying. We are as inevitable as the sunrise, *Rob*.

ROB

Here's something you need to understand, *Trent*. I am descended from a long line of Scottish warriors who *thrived* fighting people like you. My ancestors spent nearly every moment of their lives aggravating and provoking every lord and army stupid enough to skip onto their land and plant their pretty flags. You and your company may shine your shoes and wave your pretty pieces of paper, but you're no different. My ability to take you out is imprinted in my DNA! You really think you can tell me you can take my land, from *Canada*? (*He takes the sword in his hand, levels it at TRENT.*) I tell you to try. It's *mine*.

> *The storm arrives. Lightning and thunder crashes. He raises the sword as if to attack TRENT, chases him around his living room. He spanks him on the behind with the sword and chases him out the front door with the sword as he roars.*

You tell them to come and find me here, boy! I'll be waiting for all of you right here!!

> *TRENT is gone. The storm continues. ROB takes up his glass, and goes to the window, still holding the sword. Beat. Then he goes to the phone, dials.*

ROB

Adair? It's your Dad. I need you to come home. (*Thunder*) We got a storm coming.

> *Lights down.*

Easter

A few days later. The stage expands, and lights rise on the front yard of the MacLeod ranch, where ROB'S family has raised cattle and corn for over a century. There is an enormous wrap-around porch, complete with a swing, furniture, and rocking chairs. The screen door leading into the house has the beautiful slap and squeak of summer. The porch stairs lead down into a large yards there is a picnic table and other worn yard ornaments. Planters adorn the stairs and the porch rail, and the flowers within will reflect the season of each scene. At the side of the yard is a barn, with pathways to feedlots and other outbuildings of the ranch. It is afternoon. EVAN, CAM and JANE's son, comes out the door, followed by his cousin BART, ROB's son. EVAN is holding a bucket with a nipple fitted on the bottom, designed to feed baby calves. They walk towards the barn. THERESA, BART's wife, follows them out on the porch.

THERESA

Evan! Evan, I need you to come on back to the house! Hey Bart, can you stop him please?

BART

Hold up a second Evan. *(EVAN stops, does not turn)* What's up?

THERESA

Jane's coming to pick him up. His appointment got moved up.

BART

We're just feeding the orphans, Terry.

THERESA

Jane specifically asked me to keep out of the pens!

> *ROB comes out of the house and hollers over THERESA. EVAN walks away from the noise.*

ROB

Bart! Do you know where your sister is? If you're headed out to the east pasture could you look for her and tell her to move her caboose back up to the house?

THERESA

No! Evan, come back! Bart could you go get him? He never responds to me and he's going to get filthy and Jane's going to kill me!

BART

Guys, Guys! I can only answer one person at a time. Hold up, Evan!

ROB

Well I haven't seen your sister at all yet!

BART

I saw her down by the creek this morning. I'll send her home / if I see her, Dad.

THERESA

Bart!

BART

Hey Evan, need you to head on back to the house. *(EVAN doesn't move)*

ROB

Hey, you heading out to the barn?

THERESA

Bart?

BART

What!

ROB	THERESA
Take a look at the one calf with the white blaze on her forehead—I think her eye looks a little cloudy.	I need to leave in a half hour so can you please help watch Evan while I'm getting ready? Wait! Evan! Evan come back!

BART

Yeah, I thought so too.

EVAN starts for the barn, and ROB laughs at THERESA'S frustration.

ROB

Guess Evan don't like women's work.

THERESA

Yeah that's really funny, Rob.

ROB

It is pretty funny.

BART

It's not funny.

ROB

It's a little funny.

THERESA

It's going to be hilarious when Jane sends you running down the road chasing your own head. Oh, you didn't hear she's on her way over? I think that'll be pretty funny.

ROB

Yeah, that's not funny. Okay, I'll go get him. *(Exits)*

THERESA and BART regard each other.

BART

You love me so much right now.

THERESA

So much.

BART

You see Adair yet this morning?

THERESA

Yes.

BART

What'd she say about pipeline? What's she gonna do?

THERESA

Bart, there's only so many diplomatic missions I can handle. You should hear what they're saying in town—

BART

Whoa-whoa-whoa-/whoa

THERESA

Stop it. I am not a horse. Say "whoa" to me one more time and I will kick you in the head.

Beat.

BART

Ain't it great when family comes to town?

THERESA

You're killing me.

BART

One more season.

THERESA

One more season.

BART

One more harvest, and we'll have enough.

THERESA

You promise this time?

BART

We'll get there, Terry. It is what it is. What *are* they saying in town?

THERESA

They're saying Rob's dressed up like Braveheart, patrolling the fenceline. We're *that* family everybody talks about in low whispers at the Bomgaar's. We're the village idiots.

BART

That's mighty Christian of them.

THERESA

Does any of this even matter to you?

BART

It does.

THERESA

You never show it.

BART

That's because I get along with everybody.

ROB

(*Returning*) Good, because I need you to get Evan back here. He's not listening to me.

THERESA

Is he in the pen, Rob? Tell me he's not in the pen.

ROB

He's not in the pen, Terry.

BART

Is he in the pen?

ROB

Yeah, he's in the pen.

BART AND THERESA

(In unison) Dammit!

THERESA

I'm not catching blame for this! I need to leave in 15 minutes!

BART

(Over his shoulder as exits) I've got you! I'm on it!

THERESA regards ROB. Beat.

ROB

You see Adair this morning? She say anything?

THERESA

Just small talk.

ROB

You headed out?

THERESA

Bible study. I signed up for snacks.

ROB

Bart not going anymore?

THERESA

Says he's too busy here.

ROB

Yep. So what kind of snacks you bring for folks saying you're related to the village idiot?

THERESA

Rob—

ROB

I myself'd be tempted to whip up some chocolate chip cookies and load them up with a couple boxes of Ex-Lax.

THERESA

I'm really sorry Rob. I didn't mean / for you to hear that

ROB

All good, it's all good. *(Heads up steps to enter house)* If you do see / Adair

THERESA

I'll send her back here. Rob? Do you think Adair can actually help? I mean, do you think this whole fight is worth it?

ROB

(Pauses before entering house, not unkindly) Well, Terry, I expect that's family business between me and Bart and Adair. *(Exits to house)*

> THERESA *is left outside on the porch steps. After a beat, she also exits into the house. Beat, and then* ADAIR *enters the yard. She carries a backpack. As she enters the yard, she's drawn to the planters that line the porch, the yard. She kneels, does some impromptu gardening; dead-heading, weeding, etc. As she's working,* ROB *comes out of the house. He watches her before he speaks.*

ROB

Thought you'd gone AWOL on me.

ADAIR

You've already got aphids, did you know that?

ROB

It's too early for aphids.

ADAIR

You should put zinnias or asters in here.

ROB

Well, your Mother's not here, so talk to Terry about it. Where you been?

ADAIR

Walking. It's been a while.

ROB

Didn't expect you to be rambling around all day.

ADAIR

So, I hear you've become a drunken pirate farmer.

ROB

I am not a pirate.

ADAIR

Were you swinging a sword around?

ROB

I was just showing it to the guy.

ADAIR

Did you chase him with it?

ROB

I haven't chased anybody since your mother was alive.

ADAIR

Answer the question yes or no. Did you chase him with a sword?

ROB

No! *(beat)* I spanked him with it.

ADAIR

Did / you say

ROB

I bet Rob Roy spanked many an imperialist ass before they hauled him away in chains. You look skinny.

ADAIR

So do you.

ROB

Do they *have* food in California?

ADAIR

It's great to see you too, Dad.

ROB

Did you take a look at the paperwork I sent you?

ADAIR

I did. You got yourself a fight on your hands, Dad.

ROB

Me and Hugh McGibbons were both holding out together; but now that he's caved I'm the only cockroach left on this cracker. These guys are strong-arming me.

ADAIR

That's what they do. And if you take them on yourself, they win.

ROB

Then why the hell are you here?

ADAIR

Excuse me?

ROB

I thought you said you would help me!

ADAIR

And I am. Do you want my help or not?

ROB

Yes!

ADAIR

Then let me continue. Yes, I am going to take them on, but I can't do it alone. You're up against a machine that runs on tons of money and political influence you don't have. I'm bringing a guy up here next week.

ROB

Another lawyer?

ADAIR

He represents a group here in Nebraska fighting the pipeline.

ROB

A political organization? Adair, I specifically told you I will not get involved in your politics. Jesus God, do they all carry little red books?

ADAIR

These people know how to take these guys on. Do you want to beat them or not?

ROB

Yes.

ADAIR

Then let me *finish*. You already know the cards are stacked against you. The other side is banking on you to lose your resolve.

ROB

That's never been a problem.

ADAIR

These guys *want* you punching blind! It wears you down and sets them up for a knockout. You need a team, and you need a strategy. And you will listen and follow the strategy your team lays out for you. You will not play this out like a bantam rooster strutting around and squawking at the clouds, all right? Now you nod your head that you understand what I'm about to tell you, because this is my number one rule and I promise it is a *dealbreaker*. You need to trust me. Anything less than 100% and I am *gone*. I love sticking it to entitled, smirking assholes that stack the deck and cheat the system as much as you love swatting them in the ass with sharp and pointy things; and I intend to stick it to them hard enough they don't ever come back here and fuck up anybody's else's land. Okay?

   Beat.

ROB

You're a little crabby.

ADAIR

Ten minutes into a conversation, and you're already picking a fight with me.

ROB

I called you because I knew that you would be the best person to fight for me!

ADAIR

I'm fighting for this *farm*!

   BART and EVAN have appeared.

BART

Oh yay. You're home. There is harmony. There is balance.

ADAIR

There is sarcasm.

BART

I prefer dry wit.

ADAIR

Touch of the poet. *(Steps forward to hug BART)* I missed you.

BART

(*Smiles*) No you didn't.

ADAIR

Are you writing anything these days?

BART

There's not a lot of time in the Spring. Terry submitted a few poems a couple months back. (*Motions to EVAN*) I know this guy missed you.

ADAIR

Evan. Hey there.

EVAN

Adair. You came a long way.

ADAIR

I did. (*Points at bucket*) Were you feeding the orphans? How many we got right now?

EVAN

There are four babies in the barn. There were five, but she was a downer and she died.

ADAIR

But the other four are—

EVAN

The other four are good babies. Adair, do you know what Billie says?

THERESA comes out from the porch, carrying a glass of water.

ADAIR

No, what does she say?

EVAN

(*Sings*) See saw, Margery Daw,
Margery has a new master,
She just earns a dollar a day,
Because she can't work any faster.

ADAIR

(*Nods her head. Softly*) Uff-da.

EVAN

Billie says Uff-da. (*He reaches into his pocket, and pulls out an old pocket watch on a leather thong. He holds it out towards ADAIR, who is a little shaken.*) Adair, do you want to wind Grandpa's watch?

    ADAIR nods. BART steps in.

BART

Hey Evan, we need to have a talk with Dad first. Think you could give it a good polish for now?

ADAIR

Want to watch sunset on the porch later?

EVAN

Yes.

    EVAN goes to a picnic table in the yard and sits. Takes out handkerchief from his pocket, and polishes the watch. THERESA speaks to ADAIR, offers a glass.

THERESA

Thought you might want a glass of water.

ADAIR

Thanks Terry. (*Looking over at EVAN*) It's like she's still here.

ROB

It's nice that somebody remembers.

ADAIR

What does *that* mean?

ROB

It *means* it's nice that somebody remembers.

BART

Guys.

THERESA

(Looking up in the distance) Bart.

ADAIR

You think I don't remember / anything?

BART

Guys, / come on

THERESA

(Pointing) Bart!

  BART turns to look up the road.

ROB

No, I'm wondering how far you had to go to forget.

BART

GUYS. Stop.

  BART points up the road.

ADAIR

Is that Aunt Jane and Uncle Cam?

BART

Yeah.

ADAIR

Nice truck.

ROB

Brand new! Wonder where he got the money for that.

BART

(*Swinging around to ROB*) No. We do not need this right now.

ROB

I'm not doing anything.

ADAIR

What's going on?

THERESA

They're not talking.

ADAIR

Since when.

BART

Since Trent Nichols was out here.

ADAIR

That's the pipeline guy?

BART

Yes.

THERESA

Bart?

BART

(*Moving towards EVAN*) I got him. Hey Evan, let's head over to the feedlot.

THERESA

That's not what I'm / talking about!

BART

I know! I've got you too, okay?

THERESA

Seriously! She's / going to

BART

I've got you! (*Walking past ADAIR*) It's about to get pretty loud. (*Exits*)

THERESA exits to the house.

ADAIR

(*To BART*) How bad has it got? (*To ROB*) How much do Cam and Jane know about your sword fight the other night?

ROB

Ask yourself this question, counselor. How small is this town?

ADAIR

(*Beat*) Ah.

ROB

There you go.

ADAIR

Dad, any chance you could just go in the house?

Sound of gravel crunching in the driveway.

ROB

(*Leans on his knees and grins*) Oh hell no, lady. I love when family calls.

ADAIR

And you wonder why I moved to the far end of the continent. (*Waves*) Hi there!

JANE

(*Entering*) Look at that sky filled with pigs wearing wings! Adair MacKenzie MacLeod! Just look at you!

JANE MacLEOD comes bounding into the yard, her arms open wide. Her husband, CAM MacLEOD, follows more cautiously.

ADAIR

Look at you!

JANE

(*Stops short of ADAIR and smiles big, her hands resting on her hips akimbo*) Can't do that. I'm looking at you. My girl, you are a beauty.

ADAIR

(*Akimbo arms as well*) This girl has a face that scares small children. Look at you.

JANE

This old lady has bunions the size of baseballs and whiskers popping up in strange places these days. Come here! (*Big hug*) Look around, we prettied up the place for you.

ADAIR

It's so beautiful here in springtime.

JANE

It hopes eternal. Hello Rob!

ROB

(*Smiles*) Jane.

ADAIR

(*Hugs*) Hi Uncle Cam.

CAM

Hello my favorite niece. Everything your aunt said. (*Nods gravely to ROB*) Robert.

ROB

Cameron.

Pause.

JANE

Are we really gonna have to talk about the weather 'til you're both done pouting?

ROB

I'm not pouting.

JANE

Cam, your brother just spoke in a full sentence. You got one in you?

CAM

No.

ROB

You all headed to town?

JANE

Evan's appointment got rescheduled. Thought we'd grab some burgers. Where is he?

ADAIR

He's out in the feedlot with Bart.

JANE

What? What is he doing in the feedlot? *(Hollers)* Terry? Terry, you in the house?

ADAIR

What's going on?

JANE

I specifically asked Terry to keep him here at the house. Terry!

THERESA opens the door and comes onto the porch

THERESA

Hey, Jane.

JANE

I thought you were going to keep Evan here at the house!?

THERESA

Well, I tried, Jane. But then Rob thought that—

JANE

I didn't talk to Rob, I talked to you.

THERESA

I know. But then Evan was already on his way to feed the orphans, and you know / how he is when

JANE

Yes, I do know, Terry. I also know how hard it is to get him cleaned up after he's been mucking in the feedlot. *(To CAM)* We need to let them know we'll be late.

THERESA

Rob? *(ROB studies something on the ground.)* Jane? I'm sorry to let you down.

JANE

(Smiles—Nebraska Nice) Oh, you didn't let me down at all. I'll just take care of it. Be right back. *(Exits)*

ADAIR

Hey Terry? You okay?

THERESA

(Nebraska Nice—exits) Yep! Just being the village idiot. I need to get ready for church.

ADAIR

Church?

ROB

Bible study.

ADAIR

Does Bart go too?

ROB

Just Sundays.

ADAIR

How about you?

ROB

You know better than that.

CAM

We pray for you. Still waiting for it to do some good.

ROB

Good for my soul? Good for your pockets?

CAM

(Smiling, restrained) I'm not doing this with you.

ROB

Aww, we're talking about church! You've been trying to drag me back in the fold for years.

CAM

Since Billie died, to be exact.

ROB

Well fold me on in! Lemme ask you a question. Do you consider it a Christian value to steal from your own children?

ADAIR

Dad. Stop.

ROB

Jeeze, Adair, stop being so sensitive. Your Uncle Cam knows and appreciates a good philosophical discussion. *(To CAM)* You went to seminary school! This is right over home / plate!

CAM

Ask the question, Rob.

ROB

I already did. Is it a Christian value to steal from your own children?

CAM

No!

ROB

Okay! So there's a story in the news some time back about a farmer up in North Dakota, up by them Bakken fields. This guy let them put a pipeline under his wheat field. After a spell, when he opens his door at sunrise he gets walloped in the face by a strong whiff of oil coming off his fields. So he drives out there to check and steps ankle-deep in Bakken crude. Guess how big the hole was in that pipeline? Size of a *dime*. About a million gallons of oil sopped into his wheat field like a mechanic's dirty rag. I sure hope that farmer enjoyed the check he got. Probably bought the only food his babies are ever gonna pull outta that land.

CAM

That farmer might not have had a choice.

ROB

Of course there's a choice. It is stealing from our kids to take that money!

CAM

Don't you judge me!

ROB

Hey, if you want some faceless, foreign asshole to build an ecological shitstorm under your house, have at it! I just don't want it on *my* land.

CAM

I came over here trying to smooth this whole thing out!

ROB

You sent that corporate monkey over here in the first place! You want to smooth things out? Get them out of my hair!

CAM

I can't do that. That's not how they work.

ROB

Jesus wept, it's a pipe! Stick a couple elbow joints on it and route it around me!

CAM

It's one field on the northeast side of your parcel!

ROB

That *you* gave them information on!

CAM

No-no-no, hold up! They already had the specs on your land.

ROB

Then how did they get on my land for their soil analysis? I sure didn't / let them on!

CAM

I don't give a fancy fart where you stand, Rob. You want to fight them, have at it. But you invited Trent Nichols out here, got him drunk, and chased him with a sword! You think they're going to negotiate anything with you now? You're the one that's bringing down the shitstorm!

ROB

Why did you take that money?

CAM

(*Indicates in the direction of the feedlot*) You know goddamn well why I did.

ROB

Cam, we've talked about this! There's other ways to ensure Evan is taken care of.

CAM

There is no way in hell I'm talking to you about *that* right now.

JANE, EVAN, and BART have appeared from feedlot. They listen.

ROB

Well you sure do talk pretty. You pray to God with that mouth?

CAM

You always have to have the last word! You want to talk scripture, here you go. *(He stalks away)* "He who brings trouble on this family shall inherit the wind!"

ROB

(Yells after him) You're the one that's going to inherit the wind!

CAM

Am not!

ROB

Are too! Hey Cameron! You wanna hear how much money they offered? *(Beat)* They offered me *five times over* what they gave you.

CAM can't respond. Turns his back and walks away.

ROB

(Yells after him) A greedy man brings trouble to his family, but he who HATES BRIBES shall live! Proverbs!

JANE

(Calls after him) Cam?

CAM

(Off) I'll be in the car, Jane!

JANE

What the hell just happened?

ROB

Adair started it!

ADAIR

What??

ROB

(Stomps up porch stairs) You're the one that brought up church in the first place. Nice job. And what were you thinking leaving us alone together, Jane?

JANE

I am not your referee, I am not your babysitter!

ROB

(Roars from porch) Why am I the only person in this county doing the right thing here? All of this! This is St. Kilda!

ADAIR

What are you talking about?!

ROB

St. Kilda! This is how it begins! Slow rot! One parasite! It only takes one to worm through all of us at the roots! And you just stand there complacent, blinking stupid-eyed with this slack-jawed, bovine stare that I refuse to even comprehend! *(Slams into the house)*

JANE

ROB! You still coming to Easter dinner this Sunday?

ROB

(Comes back out of the house) Yeah. *(Goes back in)*

BART

Welcome home.

ADAIR

Who is St. Kilda?

JANE

Did he just call me a cow?

ADAIR

He's worse than he's ever been.

BART

What made you all "California-judgy?" Oh, that's right. California.

ADAIR

Oh and look at you, Judge Judy. I came back here to help.

BART

That's a great idea! Could you please do that instead of poking at him like a bull in the chute?

JANE

Quit, both of you. This scrap was a long time coming and now it's done. They both have a herd to feed; fences to mend. They'll sit for dinner on Sunday, pass out in front of the TV, and be making fun of all of us by Monday. We've pulled ourselves through worse. Yeah?

ADAIR AND BART

Yeah.

JANE

So then. *(Points at porch door)* That man isn't picking his battles as much as he's charging his batteries. He needs you both more than he shows.

ADAIR

Not the first time I've heard that.

JANE

Not the last time I'll remind you. Okay, come on Evan, you ready to go to town?

EVAN

(Shies away from JANE. Rocks) No. No. No-no no no / no

JANE

(Knows this routine well—coaxing gently) Evan, we talked about this / already

EVAN

*(Escalated agitation, overlapping)*NO NO NO NO NO...

JANE stops. Gives EVAN his space.

ADAIR

Jane. We can keep Evan tonight.

JANE

Adair, I can't ask / you to

ADAIR

Sunset's coming on; we talked about winding Grandpa's watch out here.

EVAN

(Calming) Billie says watch.

ADAIR

Evan, you want to stay here tonight? Watch the sunset?

EVAN

Billie says watch. *(Sits on porch, takes out watch and polishes it)*

ADAIR

(Smiles to JANE) I'll bet you both would love a big ol' ribeye.

JANE

That does sound nice. It's been... *(Puts her arm around ADAIR and BART)* Hey, look at me. I'm surrounded by MacLeods. He'll be happier here anyway. I asked Terry to keep him here at the house.

BART

Oh God. Aunt Jane, did you come down on Terry for that?

JANE

I was disappointed, but I'm over it now.

BART

Jesus. Be right back. *(Goes into house. ADAIR and JANE are alone.)*

ADAIR

I'm here to fight the pipeline.

JANE

Doesn't change a thing.

ADAIR

I'm on Dad's side in this.

JANE

I'll always be on your side. Your Dad needs you.

ADAIR

The jury's still out on that.

JANE

Well.*(Beat. Looking out towards the fields)* You see all that baby green out there? Everything the winter buried is reaching up for light. *(ADAIR looks, and JANE watches her)* Your mom used to look out over the fields the same way. She had her special way of understanding the rhythm of things. I think you understand that a little bit.

ADAIR

I live in California.

JANE

But sometimes there's just no mistaking the connection. *(Gives ADAIR a hug)* Love you. *(Exits)*

ADAIR

Love you too.

> *Sound of a car door closing, an engine, and the car receding away down the road. ADAIR joins EVAN on the porch stairs, sits.*

ADAIR

Hey there.

EVAN

Adair, you want to wind Grandpa's watch?

ADAIR

I do. *(EVAN hands it to her, and she winds)* Evan, you've kept it so polished. You want me to start?

EVAN

Can Billie be in it?

ADAIR

You bet. *(Thinks)* Do you remember our first picnic?

EVAN

The Kingdom of Toads. We all brought our lunch boxes.

ADAIR

And Mom told us we could make our own picnic, as long as it fit in our lunch boxes. So you and I packed Oreos, and Bart packed a whole brick of Velveeta cheese.

> *The porch door opens, and THERESA comes out. She passes ADAIR and EVAN on the stairs on the way to her car.*

ADAIR

Hey Terry? I'm sorry about what happened earlier.

THERESA

It's all good.

ADAIR

Want to hang out here with some beers when you're back?

THERESA

Sounds great. I know everybody's completely... (*she waves her hand*) I heard it all inside.

ADAIR

I'll hook you up when you get home.

THERESA

I'll hold you to that. (*Exits. ADAIR watches her go.*)

EVAN

Adair, you want to know what happened at the Kingdom of Toads?

ADAIR

What happened?

EVAN

We found a magic river. It's just over the hill that way.

ADAIR

Bart and I went swimming.

EVAN

But I didn't because I don't like swimming. And Billie had me sit with her. And there were so many toads in that river, Adair. There were so many—

BART comes out to the porch with two bottles of beer. He sits on the stairs with ADAIR, and hands her one.

EVAN

There were so many, you and Bart made a kingdom for them out of sticks and sand—

ADAIR

And we put as many as we could into the castle we built for them. But then they started to escape, and Bart and I fought over the biggest one. I said it was mine, and Bart said it was his.

BART

It *was* mine.

EVAN

And then the toad died. It died.

ADAIR

We held onto him too tightly.

EVAN

You were crying because it died.

ADAIR

Yes. And then Mom—

EVAN

Billie helped you bury him.

ADAIR

And we all said a prayer over him. We told him we were sorry.

EVAN

And then Billie told us all to lay back and look up at the sky.

ADAIR

She did. And we looked up at the clouds. And mom told us—

EVAN

That God is up there. Watching us. And that underneath this sky, everything is fragile.

ADAIR

And that we need to take care of all the fragile creatures.

EVAN

And that he expects us all to share.

ADAIR

All the land and water we can see beneath this sky will be for you and for Bart and for me.

EVAN

One day, this magic river and The Kingdom of Toads will belong to all of you.

Silence. The sun sets. They drink their beers, looking out over the fields.

Lights down.

Ascension

A few days later. EVAN comes around the corner of the house, with a basket of laundry from the line. He takes it to the picnic table, and begins to fold clothes. He does this with precision and discipline. As he works, he sings.

EVAN

A mighty fortress is our God
A bulwark never failing
Our helper he amid the flood
Of mortal ills prevailing.

BART enters from around the barn. He watches EVAN for a moment, and then joins him in folding. He joins in with EVAN, singing along with him. There's an easy familiarity to their signing as they work.

EVAN AND BART

For still our ancient foe
Doth seek to work us woe
His craft and power are great—

ROB and ADAIR enter from the other side of the yard, bickering. As their bickering intensifies, so does EVAN'S discomfort as he sings. EVAN begins to rock back and forth.

ROB and ADAIR stop. They look at BART. EVAN still rocks, but sings softly once shouting is over. His agitation ebbs. He picks up the laundry basket and heads back into the house, singing.

ADAIR

He still sings that.

BART

It was Mom's favorite. You telling Dad how to run this place again?

ROB

That's exactly what she's doing.

ADAIR

Oh good, you're taking his side again.

BART

Well, I only do the actual work around here, so I thought my opinion might be worth something.

ADAIR

I'll bet Dad lets you do the planter boxes.

BART

How about you actually dig in and pull your own weight before telling us what / to do

ADAIR

You think I'm not pulling my own weight? Did you go to law school?

ROB

Both of you knock it off! I know what's best for this place, and if it isn't done right, well then that's entirely my ass!

CAM has appeared from the side yard with MAT. He clears his throat.

CAM

I found your lawyer.

MAT

Hello.

CAM

He showed up at our place instead.

MAT

The sign just said MacLeod.

CAM

Thought I'd bring him by.

MAT

Thanks again.

CAM

You bet. *(Waves over his shoulder.)* Best of luck to you, Mr. Salinas!

ADAIR

(Walks up to him, offering her hand) Mr. Salinas, I'm so sorry. Adair MacLeod.

MAT

Nice to finally meet you in person.

ADAIR

This is my dad, Robert MacLeod. My brother Bart. Guys, this is the attorney I told you about, Mat Salinas.

BART

Nice to meet you.

ROB

Salinas?

MAT

Yes. Please call me Mat.

ROB

A Mexican lawyer?

MAT

Yes. That is where my family's from.

ROB

Huh.

MAT

Is that an issue?

ADAIR AND BART

(In unison) NO.

ROB

Are you a politician?

MAT

I work for an organization / that's helping

ROB

None of this is about politics. I just want these pipeline people to leave me alone. I don't want to be some poster child for a cause like some kid from the Easter Seals. I'm a humble man.

ADAIR and BART laugh.

ROB

What.

ADAIR AND BART

(in unison) Nothing.

MAT

I promise we won't need you on a poster. If you hire me, I'll be your lawyer when they come at you with the order of eminent domain. And they will be coming.

ROB

(to ADAIR) What about you?

ADAIR

I'm going to help Mat.

ROB

I thought you were helping me. Now I gotta pay something to
join a club?

ADAIR

It's better this way. There are other families that are / represented

ROB

Stop. Are you telling me you flew all the way back here to hang
our troubles on somebody else's clothesline?

ADAIR

Dad c'mon, you know this. I can't represent / my own family in

ROB

All our family business just out there flapping / in the wind

ADAIR

It's unethical for me to represent my own family. I know you
know this!

ROB

Stop talking to me like I'm addled. I guess I'll speak to who's in
charge then. *(to Mat)* So is this thing going all the way to the
Supreme Court?

MAT

Nebraska's, probably. You know what eminent domain is, right?

ROB

It's when the state can take your land for public use.

MAT

Exactly. *Public* use, like a highway or a bridge. Except in this
case, only one party benefits: a private company. Oil revenue for
Canadian Energy.

ROB

I don't understand why it's okay to take someone else's land so a company can get rich off of it. I never saw this coming.

ADAIR

(Under her breath) Of course you didn't.

ROB

Oh, you have an opinion on that?

ADAIR

No. I'm just looking at the facts.

ROB

You think I brought this on myself?

ADAIR

No. *(Beat)* But you weren't paying attention.

ROB

(Whirls on ADAIR) You got a bone to pick with me?

ADAIR

The news has been talking about this for at least a year. Did you listen? The map of the proposed line has been out there for months. Did you see it? There were public hearings. Did you go?

ROB

(Points at the fields) I'm a little bit busy from sunup to sunset if you haven't noticed. I don't / have time

ADAIR

Well mom certainly would have seen this coming, and she would have kicked your tail into town to get on top of it. It's so much easier to just be the *victim* and let everything happen to *you*, isn't it?

ROB steps right up into ADAIR's grill.

ROB

You want to talk to me about your mother? Wanna have that chat? Let's go.

ADAIR

(Beat) No.

ROB

(after a beat) Mat. I'd like you to be my lawyer. I'll pay your retainer today.

MAT

That won't be necessary.

ROB

It is and I am.

MAT

Okay.

ROB

I'm going to apologize to you for my daughter's behavior. Always been smart, but gets carried away by her emotions. I wonder if that might be a liability; not my call. I don't care about politics, I don't care about sides. Doesn't matter on what side of the fence you stand. We all drink the same water. *(Exits)*

BART

You should stay for dinner. Doesn't that sound like fun?

MAT

(Chuckles) Hey, I got time. Got an appetite too. Sounds good to me.

ADAIR

(To BART) I'm sorry.

BART

(Getting up) My wife's got a tenderloin going in there.

ADAIR

I said I was sorry.

BART

I heard you. I'll fix it. Thank you for your help, Mat. We just want control of our own destinies out here. *(Exits to house)*

ADAIR

I'd say this is the worst job interview I've ever given. *(They smile.)*

MAT

I will say there's a lot of passion in your conviction. You okay?

ADAIR

I'm fine. Listen, all of that wasn't just … *(she can't find the words)*

MAT

Something else was in there broadcasting at a higher frequency.

ADAIR

That's a good way of putting it.

MAT

If it helps, this is happening in all the families we represent. It tunes up a lot of… old frequencies. Families feel abandoned and powerless. One day a piece of paper arrives, and they're told fighting back will never matter. I bet you see that with your clients.

ADAIR

I tell my clients: all you need to fight back is one person to stand up for you.. You have to have faith in that.

MAT

Your CV is full of cases like those. I will also say that if I were sitting on the witness stand facing a cross-examination from you? I'd feel like a junebug looking up at a shoe coming down.

ADAIR

(*Smiles*) I don't like to lose.

MAT

So? (*ADAIR shakes his hand. They smile.*)

MAT

Welcome to the trenches.

Lights down.

May Day

Afternoon. The flowers in the porch planters reflect the brightness and beauty of Nebraska in late spring. The MacLeod porch and picnic table are both set for a festive picnic. From within the house, sounds of boisterous yells and laughter are heard. The screen door slams open and THERESA runs down the steps into the yard. BART comes running after.

THERESA

Bart! Stop it! Oh my God, will you stop? Knock it off!

BART

(Leaning on porch railing) Woman, get back up here on this porch.

THERESA

Absolutely not! You're insane!

BART

It's not my fault. The aroma in here has stolen my good sense; and left only bad intentions. *(He stalks her, walking down the porch stairs)*

THERESA

(Keeping the distance between them, she laughs) Are you drinking already?

BART

Do you smell that? It's maddening. It's set my hunger aflame! *(He lunges for THERESA, and she dodges, laughing.)* My favorite dish—prepared for me by my favorite dish.

THERESA

It's your mother's recipe and I make them for you every year

BART

(Stalking her again) Don't talk to me about my mother right now; there's wooing to be done. My wife, my wife, she is the best; she is the best cook in the west; we eat them all, and then we sprawl, because she makes the best—

THERESA

(Interrupting) No! God, please don't say it! Don't say it! *(BART catches her and lifts her into his arms, roaring and laughing in mock triumph)*

BART

HAM BALLS!!

THERESA can't help but laugh.

BART

A recipe writ in the South, Ham balls melt inside my mouth. The boys in town all come to call, to gaze upon my wife's ham balls!

THERESA

(Giggling as he sets her down. She stays close to him.) That sounds blasphemous.

BART

I'm all for blaspheming. *(He leans closer to her)*

THERESA

Since when did your poetry become so elementary?

BART

You really know how to charm a guy.

THERESA

I hear a lot of Dr. Seuss these days. I miss your verse, that's all.

BART

I'm averse to the verse. It's immersed with a curse. It's perverse, it's terse, and puts no money in my purse.

THERESA

Nice. When's the last time you submitted anything?

BART

When's the last time *you* submitted anything?

THERESA

I sent some pieces to NebraskaLand a couple weeks ago.

BART

I didn't know about that. Have I seen them?

THERESA

I'm a little shy about them. Look, Can we just talk about your poetry sometime?

BART

There once was a farmer's wife…

THERESA

Forget it. *(She picks up silverware and starts to place it around the table)*

BART

With a wit as sharp as a knife. She'd wield it with skill, slicing her lover's goodwill—

BART'S last verse is cut off by ROB coming out on the porch. ADAIR and EVAN follow him out, bringing dishes and napkins. They go about setting the table.

ROB

Hey Terry? Where's my white dress shirt?

THERESA

It's hanging in your closet.

ROB

No, it's not there.

THERESA

Yes, it is. I ironed it for you this morning.

ROB

It's my dress shirt.

THERESA

Which is why I ironed it for you this morning. Did you really look?

ROB

Of course I did. I'm telling you it's not there.

THERESA

Well, you need to look again.

ROB

It's my favorite shirt, Terry! Jeeze!

THERESA

(Exasperated. Exits) Seriously, Rob. How do you even put on your pants in the morning? Do you just stumble into them somehow? (Slams door)

ROB

(Following) I know where my pants are! (Slams door)

  ADAIR chuckles softly.

BART

What?

ADAIR

Nothing. I just imagined Dad having the same argument with Terry in his boxer shorts; jumping up and down, screaming for his pants.

BART

Oh no that's really happened.

ADAIR

Shut up.

BART

You shut up.

ADAIR

Your wife is a saint. How do you put up with it?

BART

(Reaches into a pocket and pulls out a flask) I talk to Uncle Jack.

ADAIR

(Smiles) Such a good man, Uncle Jack. Think I could have a heart-to-heart as well?

BART

Let's have some group therapy. *(Hands her the flask. They sit side by side and drink. EVAN continues to set the table behind them.)* So. You've invited a gentleman caller to the family shindig.

ADAIR

I work with Mat.

BART

You say that a lot.

ADAIR

Because I work with Mat.

BART

So your relationship with him is strictly professional.

ADAIR

Yes.

BART

Something you'd describe as collegial. Reciprocal accord.

ADAIR

Yes.

BART

Because you work with Mat.

ADAIR

Yes. I work with Mat. Are you hard of hearing? I work with Mat.

BART

And yet you're not working today.

ADAIR

Oh.

BART

You are a shitty lawyer.

ADAIR

Shut up.

BART

You shut up. I'm better than you.

ADAIR

I swear to God—

BART

God loves that I schooled you at your own game. I smote you.

ADAIR

(Taking the flask) Apparently I need some more career counseling from Uncle Jack.

BART

So do I, sister. So do I. *(Looks up the road)* Behold! Yonder crew-cab running apace with what beseems to me a car disguised as a shoe. The suitor of my sister drives a shoe?

ADAIR

(Recognizing MAT'S car. She stands up.) So. Yeah. Um. Hey—

BART

You talk good word things and stuff.

ADAIR

Stop it. I need to get back in the kitchen. *(Gets to door and turns back.)* Hey Bart? I'd appreciate it if... could you—

BART

I won't let him know I beat you on cross.

ADAIR

Thank you. You're a lifesaver. *(Goes inside)*

BART

It's what I do. *(Takes another drink as ROB comes outside, wearing his dress shirt)*

ROB

Bart, are you drinking already?

BART

Dad, was your shirt in the closet?

ROB

(Relents) Just pace yourself. *(Calls out)* Hey there! Is that my lawyer carrying over a box of hooch? Is that legal?

MAT

(Entering) I brought cookies with hooch. That makes it okay. Thanks for the invitation, Rob. Bart, how you doing?

BART

Doing great.

CAM and JANE enter, carrying dishes as well.

JANE

Happy May Day! Where's Evan?

ROB

He's helping inside. Cameron! Stay away from my lawyer!

CAM

Aw, has your charm worn off already? Good to see you again, Mr. Salinas.

ROB

Mat, keep your eye on this guy. He's sneaky.

MAT

(Laughing) Please, call me Mat.

JANE

Bart!

BART

Aunt Jane!

JANE

(Old game) Bartholomew-Peter-Alexander-Jonathan-Livingston-Seagull-Bruce-MacLeod!

BART

(Points back at her) Aunt Jane!

JANE

Get over here and take a look at this. I made something special! *(Lifts the cover off her dish)*

BART

(Looking inside) Whoa-ho! Ham balls falling from the sky! May I?

JANE

You bet you may! *(BART bites into one)* How'd I do? *(BART: thumbs up)* Now, I know that Billie's recipe is the holy grail, but I just thought I'd add some molasses to the glaze, and some horseradish might give it a little extra kick—

She stops. THERESA is standing on the porch with her own platter of ham balls. ADAIR is behind her.

JANE

Terry! Happy May Day!

THERESA

Hi.

JANE

Oh, did you make ham balls too? I couldn't remember.

THERESA

I make them every year.

JANE

Whoops! I'm sorry. Is it OK if we have two versions this year? Bart, you don't mind, do you?

BART is still chewing. He looks between THERESA and JANE—who to choose? The moment becomes awkward.

JANE

(Starts to wrap her dish back up) Well. I'm sorry. I'll just take this back to the car.

THERESA

No, Jane, it's fine.

JANE

I just thought it would be *fun* to have a little different recipe.

THERESA

No, no worries at all. It's fine.

JANE

Are you sure you don't mind?

THERESA

Nope. It's all fine. *(Puts down platter)* What a fun idea. I'll go get the salad. *(Heads to house)*

ADAIR

I'll help you. *(Waves to Mat)* Hey there! *(Enters house)*

JANE

I can help too!

THERESA

NO. *(She and ADAIR exit)*

> *JANE re-uncovers her dish, futzes with the tablescape. CAM walks over to ROB and BART.*

CAM

Hey. Brought you a present. *(Opens his jacket and reveals a bottle of very fine single-malt scotch)*

ROB

You wily so-and-so. *(Holds the bottle, regards it.)* Hello, old friend.

BART

Hello indeed. We should all have a toast. I'll get the glasses. *(Runs up to the house)*

JANE

Where did you get that, Cam? *(CAM opens his jacket like a flasher. JANE laughs)*

ROB

Mat? You a scotch man?

MAT

Sure am.

ROB

Then you picked a fine day.

> *EVAN emerges from the house, holding a vase of flowers.*
> *THERESA and ADAIR carry out the last of the food, followed*
> *by BART, carrying handfuls of small whisky glasses, which get*
> *distributed.*

JANE

Evan! Look at those pretty flowers!

EVAN

They're for Billie. (*He takes the flowers to the table and places them*
carefully in the center.)

ADAIR

I can't believe we have peonies blooming already.

EVAN

Billie's flowers.

JANE

They look lovely. Cam, want to help me get Evan situated here?

CAM

You bet. (*They help EVAN get a plate, and seated at the table.*)

ADAIR

(*To MAT*) Thanks for coming out. I'm glad you could make it.

MAT

I'm grateful for the invitation. I miss celebrating May Day.

ADAIR

Did you deliver May baskets? Ring the bells?

MAT

(*Laughs*) I liked getting caught and kissed, actually.

BART

(*Laughs*) So did Adair!

ROB

(*Pouring whisky into everyone's glasses*) Back in the old country, this day was called Bealtaine.(*Pronounced: Be-al-te-nah*) Our clan, the MacLeods, spent this day welcoming the season of growth. In those days, they drove the herd between two enormous bonfires. We don't do that, but we still mark the day. Adair and Bartholomew's mother made our own family traditions. She left treats in our lunch pails; flower chains in the breezeway. Those were her bonfires. And she kept her herd good and safe. (*Raises his glass, and the rest follow*) Happy May Day to you, Billie. We all still flourish and thrive. Slainté.

ALL

(*Echo and drink*) Slainté!

EVAN

You know what Billie says?

ROB

What's that, Evan?

EVAN

Come Lord Jesus be Thou our guest may these thy gifts to us be blessed Amen.

Pause.

ROB

Amen.

CAM

Well, how about that. Made you pray, you old pagan.

All laugh, take their places around the table, if they haven't already. Dinner scenes are always a fiasco—apologies from the playwright.

CAM

Billie is still the only person that gets you right with God.

ROB

Well, God had a chance to make that right himself, didn't he? Maybe if you'd stayed in the seminary, you'd be more convincing in your case.

MAT

Wait. You were going to be a minister?

ROB

We'd be calling him Captain Holy Smoke or something if it weren't for Jane sashaying into his life and leading him into sin—

JANE

Rob MacLeod, will you stop telling tall tales? Cam, tell him I did not lead you into sin.

CAM

Jane didn't lead me into sin, everybody.

JANE

Thank you.

CAM

She couldn't lead, because she has no sense of direction. The night she and I went out to the old bridge in my Dad's pickup, I did all the driving. (*Chorus of "Ew's" and "We don't want to hear this"*) I go to church regular to make up for it now. And I thank the Lord every day. (*Kisses JANE'S hand*)

JANE

(*To ROB*) You should be grateful for that year he spent in seminary. It gave him the patience to forbear all your drama.

ROB

He's my brother. He has to forbear me.

CAM

(Laughing) That's right! To not forbear is forbidden! *(Pointing to ROB)* Mat, did you know this guy was going to be a lawyer?

MAT

I had no idea! What changed your plans?

ROB

Life happened. Hard to walk away from the farm when it needs you.

BART

I'll drink to that.

MAT

(To BART) Did you study law as well?

BART

No, I chose a lower path.

THERESA

That's not true.

BART

I would have made a lousy preacher, so I came back here instead.

THERESA

Bart was on his way to Iowa City for his MFA. He's an amazing poet.

BART

And he doesn't even know it!

THERESA

He's a very talented writer.

BART

He's a very talented farmer.

JANE

Mat, did you go to school here in the state?

MAT

My whole life. Anybody would be hard-pressed to convince me to leave.

CAM

Why is that?

MAT

Something about living here stays in your bones. I think it's because something in me is connected to how this land marks the passing of time. Do you ever notice how time seems to stop right before a thunderstorm blows through?

ADAIR

Or how you know spring's coming because the sandhill cranes are flying overhead.

JANE

Lightning bugs in June.

THERESA

Cicadas in July.

CAM

Do you ever notice how flocks of black starlings all fly in those beautiful formations in the autumn? Like schools of fish up there in the sky.

BART

It's called murmuration. Mom always said it was magic.

ADAIR

People razz me all the time about living in "flyover" country; this
endless, bleak expanse they roll their eyes at from their airline seats.

CAM

(Snorts) Flyover country. I say, let 'em keep flying over; they don't
know.

JANE

I'm fine keeping all this beauty to myself.

BART

(In his own world)
I run into the darkness of the storm
In search of her light's emergence—
Blue, bruised curtains lumber behind, trudging eastward
As heaven spreads her fingers of infinite light.
Flora and fauna stretch upward, closed-eyed, bathing in warmth
Down to me, under dripping eaves, wiping water from my cheeks.
I walk forward into her light, tiny pinholes of blue sky
Searching for her in this holy silence of a world reborn, returned.
In this moment I am Kharon, fighting currents from both shores
Flailing to anchor my raft and hold my balance—
Reaching upward as clumsy as a four-year-old boy
For apron strings, and arms to lift me once more
Surrounded in softness, shelter, and warm cinnamon.

> Pause. No one knows what to say. BART raises his glass silently
> to the sky and drinks.

ADAIR

That was beautiful.

MAT

It was. (He looks to the sky) So many cycles of life and rebirth
here. Endless wonder from horizon to horizon. It's why I love
living here. We see change approaching in the distance, and so

we prepare. Living here, we've learned to become resilient, but most importantly, *reliant*. We lean on our family, we're there for our neighbors, and we revere how important it is to tolerate our differences.

CAM

(*Shrugs*) There's bigger things to worry about.

ROB

Gotta forbear.

MAT

Exactly.

ROB

(*Pointing at ADAIR*) She's still a Communist, though.

> *Everybody laughs.*

ADAIR

I'm forbearing the hell out of you right now.

ROB

Tell me you don't miss all this.

ADAIR

I'm back here, aren't I?

JANE

I've always thought you'd be a great farmer. Your mom did too. She did!

CAM

(*Scottish brogue*) Ah now! Lassie! Ye would be right fine mucking o' the byre would she not, Robert brother mine?

ADAIR

(*She knows what's coming*) Oh No. No-no-no-no—

ROB

(Scottish brogue—points at ADAIR) By God! Cameron brother mine that's a fact be true! Bart! You get up here and do right by your forefathers!   CAM Your foreBEARS!

ADAIR, THERESA, AND JANE

A chorus of "No, not again!" and "Don't!" and "Stop, for the love of God!"

ROB AND CAM

(Full-on Braveheart roars) YES, BY GOD WE WILL!!!!

ROB and CAM then begin their own tipsy traditional rendition of "The Mucking' o' Geordie's Byre." They sing it with the best Scottish accents, stamping their feet, clapping, and immersing themselves in the raucous joy of the song. At some point, BART joins them, and they lock arms and sing loud to the sky in full voices. EVAN rises from his seat and moves to a corner of the table farther away, to get away from the noise.

ROB AND CAM AND BART

(Finishing the song)
For the grain was tint, the besom was deen
The barra widna row its leen
An' sicken a soss it never was seen
At the muckin' o' Geordie's byre!

JANE

(Has stepped away from the group—looking up the road) Cam? You know that car coming up the road?

CAM

(Looking out) Nope. (To ROB) Should I?

ROB

(Looking out) The guy from the pipeline had a blue car.

BART

(*Looking out*) Trent Nichols. That's his car. (*Looks at ROB*) Jesus
Christ, you're drunk again.

ROB

So are you. (*ADAIR starts to talk, ROB cuts her off*) It's okay. Mat,
you think this is it?

MAT

I do.

ROB

Then I got my lawyers with me. Cam, you and Jane and Evan may
want to head out.

CAM

We're staying.

ADAIR

Dad, you want us to do the talking?

ROB

I'll tag you in if I need you. (*He watches the distance.*) Hell of a
thing. (*They all stand together, watching the car approach.*)

   Sound of a car door slamming. TRENT enters and faces the
   Family MacLeod.

TRENT

Afternoon, Mr. MacLeod. Bart. Theresa.

THERESA

Hello.

TRENT

I'm sorry to interrupt. I didn't realize there was a family
celebration today.

ROB

What can we do for you, Trent?

TRENT

I thought it would be better to bring this in person. *(Holds up an envelope)* Mr. MacLeod, this is official paperwork to condemn 20 acres of your property to complete the construction of our pipeline.

ROB

It's not your land to take.

TRENT

I'm sorry. This is what it comes to. Rob, the offer I gave you still stands. If you dig in for a fight, it will make no difference.

ROB

Adair.

ADAIR

Dad.

ROB

Tag.

ADAIR

(Steps forward and accepts the envelope from TRENT—hands it to MAT) Mr. Nichols, my name is Adair MacLeod. Consider this notice that tomorrow morning, we will be filing for an injunction against your company's claim. We will also be naming you in our suit.

TRENT

Wait. You're filing a case against *me*?

MAT

(Stepping forward, offering his hand) Mr. Nichols, my name is Mat Salinas—

TRENT

I know who you are.

MAT

Excellent. Is this your signature?

TRENT

Yes, but I only work / for the

MAT

Welcome to the party, Mr. Nichols.

TRENT

Rob, these people are only interested in getting themselves on the TV news. They can't help you. It won't make any difference.

CAM

Trent, there has to be another way. Can't we get some engineers in here to figure out how to go around him? He's got a right to say no.

TRENT

The governor's approved the route. The soil on this land is the composite we want.

ROB

And who the hell let you on my land in the first place? I already know it wasn't Cam. Were you trespassing?

TRENT

Bart?

Everyone turns to BART. There's a shocked silence.

BART

I'm sorry, Dad. I didn't see any harm letting them on to take samples.

ROB

Bart. What were you thinking?

BART

I don't know! I'm sorry! I didn't know what would happen!

ROB

How could you not know that when you let people like this onto your property, they always have other motives in mind? *Damn it, whose side are you on?*

ADAIR

Dad, /please

BART

There is nothing wrong with trying to be a good neighbor!

TRENT

I'm telling you, it won't make any difference—

ROB

(*Interrupting*) Trent, if I hear you say nothing makes a difference one more time I swear to god I will drop-kick your ass back / to your car

TRENT

(*Interrupting*) It's not me! It's my company! I just work for them!

ROB

(*Enraged*) You shook my hand! You think a handshake is just a quaint little *thing*? One of those folksy finger-waves we give as we drive by on the highway? Bullshit! When you shake my hand, it's not just your honor you pledge, boy. It's your *name*. Your *people*. You pledge to honor his family—and they pledge the same back to you and *yours*. Who are you even *connected* to? A bunch of slick suits that have never set foot in this country! But you'll do as you're told, turn us out, and then deny them faster than Peter at sunrise!

TRENT

I'm sorry, / I really

ROB

(*Interrupting*) And now you're *sorry!?* How in God's name am I
fighting someone as feeble and feckless as this? If you're going
to take my land, stand tall and look me in the face! Tell me what
you're doing is fair! Face me! / Face me!

> *As ROB's speech gets more strident, EVAN claps his hands over*
> *his ears and rocks and sings ever louder.*

EVAN

A mighty fortress is our God a bulwark never failing for still our
ancient foe doth seek ...

JANE

Evan? (*Goes to him*) It's all right, baby. Where's your watch? Cam?

THERESA

I saw him put it in his shirt pocket.

EVAN

TO WORK US WOE HIS CRAFT AND POWER OH NO OH
NO / OH

JANE

Evan? Let's get out the watch. Cam!

THERESA

I can get it! I got it! (*Reaches over to EVAN'S shirt pocket, grabs*
watch) Evan? Let's get out your / watch, okay?

EVAN

NO NO NO NO NO NO!!!

> *EVAN reaches full meltdown, and his arm flies out to brush*
> *Theresa away, hitting her in the face. She falls back. His arms*
> *fly in front of him, and all the dishes, glasses, and food fly*
> *everywhere. He begins to hit himself. JANE and CAM get*

on either side of EVAN and restrain him, keeping him safe.
Suddenly, EVAN begins to seize.

JANE

Cam! He's seizing!

CAM

Okay, let's get him on the ground. You got him?

JANE

Got him.

JANE and CAM lower EVAN to the ground swiftly and gently.
They loosen his collar, and roll him on his side. When he's secure,
they stand back.

TRENT

(Approaches) Should I call somebody?

JANE

Step back. Let him have his space please.

CAM

He'll stop. Give him time.

Pause. BART goes to help THERESA up off the ground.

ADAIR

Terry? You okay?

THERESA

(Standing, a bit shaken. She is covered in dirt and food.) I thought if
he had his watch it would help.

JANE

It didn't.

THERESA

I'm sorry.

CAM

Terry, this wasn't your fault.

BART

Once he starts on that road, it's not going to change.

JANE

Here, he's coming back. *(Kneels over EVAN)* There you are. Hi there, baby. Can we get you to sit up? *(She helps him sit up gently)* Rob, can we clean him up inside?

ROB

Yeah, let me get the water started. Mat? Can you help?

MAT

(Follows) You bet.

EVAN

(Slow. He cannot form words well, but tries to ask for Billie) Buuuuuh…

JANE

(Easing him up to standing) It's okay, Evan. I've got you. Mama's here.

EVAN

Buuhie? Want Buuhie.

JANE

I know, I know. We need to clean up right now.

EVAN

NO. *(Pushes her hand away)* WANT BUUHIE… *(JANE stands up, backs away.)*

ADAIR

(Kneels to EVAN) Evan? Do you want to talk about Billie? We can inside.

EVAN

Yes. Buuhie.

They help EVAN onto his feet, and start to walk him towards the house. JANE follows behind.

ADAIR

Bart? Can you get me Grand-dad's watch?

BART

(Taking it from THERESA and walking towards the house) Got it. *(He follows JANE into the house)*

ADAIR

(As they all exit) Did you know that when Bart and I were kids, Mom would tell us it was time to make dirt rings in the tub? We would have contests to see who left the dirtiest one...

The screen door closes. THERESA and TRENT are left alone in the yard. THERESA finds a trash bag, and begins to clean up.

TRENT

I am so sorry.

THERESA

It's okay.

TRENT

I had no idea that would happen. Was it my fault?

THERESA

No. He just does sometimes.

TRENT

Can I... Can I help you, Theresa? It might make it go easier.

THERESA

Sure. Thank you.

TRENT grabs a trash bag. They work together in silence for a moment.

TRENT

I saw you trying to help. Why did he need the watch?

THERESA

When Evan was a child, Billie was the only one that could calm him down. She gave him that watch, and taught him how to take care of it. When Evan would get agitated, she would ask him to give it to her, wind it, and tell him a story. It gave him a path back to the family, if that makes any sense.

TRENT

Did you know her well?

THERESA

Billie? Oh, yes. When she got sick, we moved back here to help out.

TRENT

Cancer?

THERESA

Yes. By the time they realized they'd misdiagnosed, it was too far advanced. Rob could barely function. He wanted to sue the doctors, the hospital… And then after he and Adair had their blow-up, it just made sense for me and Bart to stay on.

TRENT

He wanted Adair to sue the doctors?

THERESA

He wanted Adair to convince Billie to—(*she stops herself, reflects*) Sometimes, I think people have to follow their own path. Holding them back can almost be a sin, you know?

TRENT

I understand.

THERESA

She was the kindest person I have ever met. She made me feel so welcome here—a part of this place. Have you ever seen someone that has a brighter light about them? As if they're somehow lit from within? And when they speak to you, their light shines on you? Like grace?

TRENT

Yes.

THERESA

That was Billie. I miss her.

Lightning flashes from afar. They both look towards the horizon.

TRENT

What do you think? About a half-hour away?

THERESA

(Nods) Mmmhmm.

Long, low roll of thunder in the distance. They resume their work.

TRENT

I meant to tell you… You've got a little spot of blood there—by your lip. *(He points to his own)* About right there?

THERESA

Oh. I must have bit it.

TRENT

Does it hurt?

THERESA

I can't feel a thing. *(Laughs quietly)* I'll bet I look monstrous. Ham balls are all the fashion these days.

TRENT

(Laughs) All the men will follow you.

THERESA

All the dogs, cats, raccoons…

TRENT

Coyotes will be howling outside your window at night.

THERESA

Yeah… right.

They regard each other. Pause.

TRENT

Theresa. I know I've brought this trouble to your family. To you. I really am trying to do the right thing.

THERESA

I know it wasn't an easy decision, coming out here in person.

TRENT

It was hard to stand there facing them—so far on the outside.

THERESA

I know how that feels. You've always been kind to me.

TRENT

You've always been kind to me. I've enjoyed our talks after Bible study.

THERESA

I didn't know people walked people to their cars anymore. I look forward to that.

TRENT

Maybe I look forward to it too much.

They approach each other, but stop when it gets too close.

THERESA

I love that you call me by my full name.

TRENT

It's how I see you.

THERESA

Trent…

TRENT

I know, I know. I'm sorry—

THERESA

No. That's not what I was going to say. I just know I can't take one more step forward right now. Because I know it will be the end of me.

TRENT

That light you were talking about earlier, Theresa? I see it in you.

Lightning in the distance. Neither of them moves. The thunder rolls a little sooner, louder.

THERESA

Will you be there on Wednesday?

TRENT

Yes.

Lightning flashes.

THERESA

Thank you for all your help tonight, Trent. I can't tell you how much I appreciate it.

TRENT

You're welcome. Theresa.

TRENT turns and walks to his car. THERESA watches him go. Thunder rolls. She regards the house. As she walks up to the house, the storm gets closer.

~ END OF PART ONE ~

PART
TWO

Memorial Day: Morning

Morning sun appears on the MacLeod farm. There is tranquil silence. There are flowers around the porch that align with the season. It's a gorgeous early summer morning, and you can hear the gentle sound of the wind and birdsong. From within the house, sounds of fighting are heard. Suddenly, THERESA slams open the screen door and runs away from the house. She is still in her pajamas, disheveled, and wild-eyed. She holds her car keys in her hand. BART follows her at the same rate of speed. He holds a piece of paper in his hand.

BART

How long!? Answer the question!

THERESA

I'm sorry. I'm so sorry, Bart...

BART

How *long*, Terry? How long has this been happening?

THERESA

A few weeks. We just started talking more at church. It just / happened.

BART

At church. You're having an affair with Trent Nichols. At *church*?

THERESA

I'm sorry.

BART

Don't say you're sorry. Tell me why.

THERESA

Bart…

BART

Why. Why do I have to find out about this in a love letter. From *Trent*?

THERESA

Bart, I'm so / sorry

BART

I'm your husband. You're / my wife!

THERESA

Please!! Stop yelling at me…

BART

ARE YOU SERIOUS??? *(THERESA turns to go to the car)* Okay… okay. Terry wait! Just wait… just. Just let me… Please stay. Please talk to me. *(THERESA stops)* Okay? Listen, I need to get my head around this. I have questions. Will you answer them?

THERESA

(After a beat) Yes.

BART

He says you're the most beautiful woman he's ever met. And that he can't wait to see you again after Bible study. Under the old bridge. That's where you meet?

THERESA

Yes.

BART

The old bridge. Our bridge.

THERESA

Yes.

BART

What do you do when you meet Trent under the old bridge?

THERESA

We talk.

BART

What else? *(THERESA can't answer)* What else, Terry? You have to answer. This is how this *works*.

THERESA

Yes, we kiss! Okay? We kiss!

BART

You kiss. What else? Does it go farther?

THERESA

(Whisper) Yes.

BART

Yes?

THERESA

(Nods her head) Yes.

BART

Jesus… He says that he thinks he loves you. Well?

THERESA

I don't know.

BART

(Roars) BULLSHIT!

THERESA

(Roars back) I SAID I DON'T KNOW! Sometimes you just don't know. There are so many things I don't know, Bart! The whole world is exploding right now.

BART

You can't tell me you don't / know how you

THERESA

(Interrupting) I know I have been unhappy, all right? I've been carrying it for a long time. I thought I could just wait it out. Bury it, cover it up. Just go about my days. I prayed and prayed and prayed for things to change, and waited for the change to happen. But I didn't know it would / happen like this

BART

How long have you been praying?

THERESA

I didn't realize what I was doing was just burying an enormous charge under everything, and I can't put the pin back in the grenade! There's only one thing I know for certain right now. There is another life out there for me. I keep seeing signs. There are signs everywhere, Bart, and I have to follow them. I can't explain it any better. God knows I deserve His punishment for what I've done to you. But I'm ready for those consequences too. This isn't my life. I don't belong here.

BART

You belong with me.

THERESA

I've broken my vows.

BART

We can get past it. This is us. Is it because we live here? Is it Jane? Is it because … is it because of having kids?

THERESA

Those are symptoms of the whole sickness. We stopped, Bart. We
stopped taking care of ourselves. We got lazy and we quit.

BART

Speak for yourself. I never quit on you. I promised to take care of
you and I have. I never quit on us.

THERESA

Yes, you did.

BART

Excuse me??

THERESA

This is Rob's life.

BART

You and me / agreed all about

THERESA

This is not your life! You never even think of writing / anymore

BART

No-no-no this is all new to me. You never told me you were
unhappy. You *never* told me your happiness hinged on whether or
not I kept *writing* / after long days

THERESA

How could you *not* see me struggling? How many times did we
talk about moving away to town? How many times did we bury
something away until the next season? And then the next, and
then the next? There's always another season, but nothing ever
grows!

BART

You keep giving me all these excuses…

THERESA

I'm giving you my reasons.

BART

What about the one where you promised to stay with me forever?
All this back-breaking *bullshit* I deal with every day has been for
us... you can't just walk away. *(The fact that she is leaving finally
sinks in.)* This isn't happening. You can't do this. You're my wife.
Theresa, *please.* I don't know how to do any of this without you
here. I can't do this without you. Don't do this to me. Don't leave
me. *(He reaches for her)*

THERESA

(Pulls away from him. Backs away.) I'm sorry. I'm so sorry,
Bart. *(She looks up. ROB is silently watching from the screen door.
THERESA meets ROB'S eyes before she turns and runs to her car)*
I'm sorry. *(Exits)*

BART

NO!!! Theresa!! Don't! Theresa!!! *(When the sound of the car
starts, BART'S despondency changes to rage.)* FUCK YOU! FUCK
YOU! YOU'RE KILLING US!

*BART gathers gravel with both hands, and hurls them after
THERESA'S car. He throws the gravel and screams until he is
spent. And then he kneels and softly sobs.*

BART

You're killing me. Oh my God... Oh my God...

*ROB stays in the doorway, watching, struggling with whether or
not to go to his son. Finally, he fades back into the house, letting
BART have his space.*

Lights down.

Memorial Day: Noon

ADAIR and MAT sit at a table on the porch. Their laptops are open.

ADAIR

Okay, read it back to me?

MAT

The legislature has the plenary power not only to grant or withhold the right to exercise the power of eminent domain, but also to define the quantum of interest or estate which may be acquired. Burnett v. Central Nebraska Public Power and Irrigation District.

ADAIR

What number listed under the arguments?

MAT

(Looking) Um… sixty three.

ADAIR

No.

MAT

No, it's not sixty-three?

BART comes around the corner of the house, and up the stairs.

ADAIR

Hey...

BART ignores her and slams into the house.

ADAIR

Sorry. What was the question?

MAT

You said "no."

ADAIR

Oh.

MAT

Argument sixty-three...

ADAIR

Right. (*She looks back at her laptop*) I don't know if you're citing the right case... (*Sound of car coming into the driveway*)

MAT

Is that Jane?

ADAIR

Umm. Yeah. (*Small beat, then she goes back to her laptop*) The reference here to plenary power... you said that was Burnett?

MAT

Yes.

JANE is walking a determined beeline across the yard to the house. ADAIR watches her approach as she continues to speak.

ADAIR

I think that should be Stenberg v. Moore. (*JANE comes up the stairs*) Hey / Aunt J-

JANE slams into the house.

MAT

Uhh... no. I think I cited that right. It's Burnett. Here's what
I have for Stenberg v. Moore: the Legislature cannot give the
Governor the authority to delegate the eminent domain authority
to another party or entity...

*BART comes slamming out of the screen door, and makes a
beeline for the barn. MAT and ADAIR watch. MAT continues.*

MAT

Doing so makes the Governor the *legislature,* not the executive—

*JANE comes slamming out of the house, wearing the flustered
look of someone that's been told, bluntly and colorfully, to mind
her own business. She marches back towards her car. MAT and
ADAIR watch her go.*

MAT

Adair?

ADAIR

Hmmm?

MAT

You doing OK?

ADAIR

Doing great!

MAT

I think not so much.

ADAIR

What do you mean?

MAT

I mean Bart. (*ADAIR tries to refute, but MAT cuts her off.*)
I stopped for gas, and the word was your sister-in-law was
hysterical in front of Trent Nichols' house this morning.

ADAIR

In her pajamas.

MAT

I heard that, too. How is Bart?

ADAIR

I've never seen him like this. He's real dark, and I'm worried.

MAT

How can I help?

ADAIR

(Sad laugh) You do any family law? (MAT takes her hand, she gently pulls it away after a small beat) Thanks. Best thing for you and me is to finish this brief—

ROB comes out onto the porch.

ROB

Adair? Did you see where Bart—?

ADAIR

(Points) Barn.

ROB

Thanks. (Heads down stairs, then turns back to ADAIR) Hey, Adair? We're getting close to noon.

ADAIR

That's true.

ROB

Well, we don't have any dinner set up yet.

ADAIR

That's probably true too.

ROB

So I need you to get that done. Let's go.

ADAIR

I'm sorry?

ROB

Dinner. It's noon, and we're going to need dinner. Terry always keeps sandwich things handy in case she has to go somewhere... so yeah. Sandwiches will be fine.

ADAIR

Well, then you can make them, Dad. I need to work on this.

ROB

(Stops. Turns.) What did you say?

ADAIR

I said I'm working on this brief. I need to work on this. You can make your own sandwich.

ROB

I don't want to make my own sandwich. I asked you to make them.

ADAIR

And I'm telling you that I'm working on this brief.

ROB

I'm not going to ask you again.

ADAIR

Then I don't need to repeat myself.

ROB

Are you telling me that you're not going to make me a sandwich. *Today?* Of all days?

ADAIR

Actually, I'm telling you that it is completely within your own power to make your own sandwich. Sandwiches are not my purview.

ROB

Your *purview?* Don't you throw big words at me like I don't know 'em. I know what purview means.

ADAIR

Excellent! Then your aptitude for vocabulary should translate nicely into the skills necessary for slicing your own bread and your own cheese.

ROB

GODDAMMIT! Make me a sandwich!

ADAIR

No, goddammit, make your own damn sandwich!

ROB

I don't make my own sandwiches!

ADAIR

Why is that?

ROB

Because I'm a... *(Stops)*

ADAIR

Because you're big king of the farm??

ROB

(Booms) Because I'm your *father!* Now you listen; I'm going out there to the barn to get your brother, who is having the worst day of his life. I'm going to tell him to come back here and build up some strength to get him to the end of this day. And then we're going to come back here and let you *work*. So nice of you to be supportive of your brother. *(Walks away)*

ADAIR

(Yells after him) What?! Do you think I just flew out here for a suntan? *(She whirls and looks at MAT.)* What?!

MAT

Nothing.

ADAIR

I'm here to bail them out of this mess! That's the only reason I'm
here!

MAT

You think he doesn't want you here otherwise?

ADAIR

He doesn't care if I'm here or not. I'm not Terry.

MAT

Why do you think he doesn't care if you're here?

ADAIR

I won't fight with him. You see what happens? The minute I stand
up for myself, I'm the one to blame. We need to be working.

MAT

Okay.

ADAIR

So let's get back to work. *(She sits. Stares off into space.)*

MAT

You're still coming up with the last word, aren't you?

ADAIR

Fuck!

MAT

(Laughs) I do it all the time. Look; I think I'm going to head back
to town.

ADAIR

I'm sorry about all this, Mat.

MAT

It's okay. Focus on your family. *(ADAIR reacts)* Hey-hey! I'm not talking about sandwiches! I'll finish up this draft, and I'll call you tonight. Sound good?

ADAIR

Sounds good.

MAT

Okay with you if I share an observation? Neutral party.

ADAIR

Sure.

MAT

I watch your Dad. It's clear he's proud of you, and I can tell that's difficult for him to express. I watch you here, and it's clear you love this place. This is your element. Let's talk tonight, okay?

ADAIR

Okay. Thank you.

MAT

See you. *(Exits)*

> ADAIR *watches him go. Then she slaps down her laptop and goes into the house as* ROB *follows* BART *out of barn.*

ROB

Bart? *Bart,* wait. That's not what I meant to say.

BART

No, that's exactly what you meant to say. So all of this is my fault; that's what you're saying.

ROB

I never said that.

BART

You said I was lazy!

ROB

I never said lazy, I said both of you were *complacent*. When you're married for a long time, sometimes you take things for granted.

BART

I do not want marriage advice from you.

ROB

All right! I'm sorry! I'll butt out.

BART

And who the hell are you to lecture me about taking things for granted? That's all you ever *do*.

ROB

You watch your tone with me.

BART

I don't have to watch shit. You've taken advantage of me and Terry for years.

ROB

What, you think farming doesn't take a little bit of *work* to make a living?

BART

What, you think I haven't broken my ass for years working on this place? When have I *ever* been lazy?

ROB

I told you, I never called you lazy!

BART

We've been nothing but free labor for you for years.

ROB

This is your farm, Bart! Why the hell did you come back here?

ADAIR has appeared on the porch.

BART

Because Mom was dying! You couldn't even take care of *yourself* after she was gone!

ROB

You could have left anytime you wanted!

BART

(Looking at ADAIR) No. Adair went ahead and took that upon herself.

ADAIR

You leave me out of this.

BART

You're such a chickenshit. You never fight your own fights.

ADAIR

I make my living fighting for shit that matters!

BART

Well, you've made it clear your family doesn't matter shit to you!

ADAIR

You both treat me like shit every time I come back here!

BART AND ROB

(In unison) You never come back here!

BART

And I never treat you like shit! You and Dad get in the same room, and I'm automatically the referee; I'm so sick of it all.

ROB

So you think I kept you prisoner here, Bart? Is that what you're saying?

BART

How many times did Terry and I talk to you about hiring Virgil or Ray back on to help out? How many times did you say "maybe next season—"

ROB

Bart, can you make the price of corn go up? I can't afford to hire help! (*Beat*) Is that why you let Trent Nichols out here?

ADAIR

Dad! Stop it!

ROB

Answer my question! Did you want to sell me out to Trent? You brought him out here. Look where that got you!

ADAIR

Leave him alone! God, why do you always have to jam your thumb into the cuts?

CAM appears around the corner of the barn. He watches unnoticed.

ROB

Oh, *now* you stand up for your brother? You were fine leaving him and me here when your Mother died!

ADAIR

You didn't want me here! You said you couldn't stand the sight of me!

ROB

Is that a reason to spend your life pouting on the other side of the country?

BART

You did. You fucking left.

ADAIR

(*To BART*) No way I was going to stay here after the way he treated me.

BART

I held this place together, and you ran away!

ROB

I needed your help. Your *mother* needed your help, and you turned on her!

ADAIR

She couldn't take the chemo! She didn't want any more of that poison in her veins, and she needed you to support her! You bullied her endlessly instead! It was her choice; she needed somebody on her side!

ROB

She was way too sick to make any decisions! You had no business sticking your nose into it!

ADAIR

I had every right to defend her decision. She was my *mother!*

ROB

She would have had more time if she'd stayed at the treatment!

ADAIR

And that's not what she chose, and you wouldn't listen! Somebody had to stand up for her!

BART

What, are you saying I didn't?

ADAIR

I didn't see you sticking up for me when Dad told me to get out!

BART

Somebody needed to look after Mom while you and Dad took everything out on each other!

ROB

You let your mother die!

ADAIR

She was already dying!

ROB

That should have been a decision between me and my *wife!* You made it all about *yourself!*

ADAIR

It was between her and *God.* She tried so hard to make you listen—

ROB

BULLSHIT! God doesn't visit hell upon the holy! She did everything a faithful follower would do for Him! And what was her reward? What was mine!? You have no idea how it feels walking these paces from sunup to sunset, and coming home to a lifeless, cold house filled with nothing but empty memories of the life she and I used to have!

Beat. ROB and ADAIR realize what's just been said. They look at BART, who says nothing. He pulls out a set of car keys, and stalks to his truck.

ADAIR

Bart, wait! Bart!

Sound of the truck speeding away. ADAIR and ROB regard each other. Then ROB walks up the stairs to the house.

ADAIR

There's sandwich shit on the sideboard!

ROB slams into the house. ADAIR collapses on the stairs as CAM approaches.

CAM

You okay?

ADAIR shakes her head. CAM sits next to her.

CAM

Do you remember the Augsberger farm down the road? Lily always brought those kolaches by in the summer? They were such an industrious bunch.

ADAIR

Are you really talking to me about *kolaches* right now?

CAM

No, I'm talking about the Augsbergers. Anyway, I went by there one time after Otto had been dipping into his apricot wine; and Lily didn't like when Otto fell off the wagon, so they were having a pretty big tiff.

ADAIR

And?

CAM

It was the most civil argument I've ever seen in my life. They were so… respectful. I didn't know people actually fought like that.

ADAIR

Your point?

CAM

(Shrugs) I just wonder what our family would be like if we were Prussian. I think I would have made a great stoic.

ADAIR

Do you ever regret staying? Did you ever tell Grandpa you wanted to leave?

CAM

We never talked back to your Granddad. Never. We weren't given a choice. When he needed us, we dropped everything and came home. *(He looks out to the fields)* And look at all we grew. We doubled our acres, improved our yields, and we worked hard to gain some leeway for you kids.

ADAIR

Leeway for what?

CAM

So you would have a choice. Anyways, Jane called a while ago. I know things are less than stoic around here. How about we make up some supper and bring it over around 6?

ADAIR

That would be great. *(ADAIR'S phone rings. She pulls it out.)* Jesus.

CAM

Who is it?

ADAIR

It's Terry.

Lights down.

Memorial Day: Night

*Evening. The sun has set. BART is alone, sitting on the
porch steps. There is a duffel bag at his feet. Sound of a car
approaching. Headlights shine on his face. Sound of car door
slamming. TRENT walks into the yard, and faces BART.*

BART
Wasn't expecting you.

TRENT
I know.

BART
Adair told me she talked to Terry.

TRENT
She did. She got nervous. I offered to come instead.

BART
You're a helluva guy.

TRENT
Is that her bag?

BART
Yeah.

TRENT
Just one?

BART

Yeah.

TRENT

Can I take it?

BART

Come and get it. *(Beat)* You take *everything*, don't you, Trent?

TRENT moves forward to get the bag. BART puts his foot on it.

BART

But first... *(Reaches behind him and raises a near-empty fifth of whisky)* I have some questions.

TRENT

Bart. I don't want any trouble.

BART

It's like nobody knows how to have an affair anymore. This is how it *works*. I had to explain the rules to Terry this morning too... Jesus, was that this morning? Trent, this has been a very long day.

TRENT

Yes.

BART

So. *(Takes another pull)* You started screwing my wife at church.

TRENT

Is that a question?

BART

Sorta. Here's my question. Was there any point at all when you both saw the *irony* in that? At any point did that just seem insanely ironic to you?

TRENT

Is that really ironic?

BART

Yes, it really is. It's an incongruity between the actual result of a sequence of events, and the normal or expected result.

TRENT

Okay.

BART

For example: it was a tragic irony that Trent and Terry fornicated themselves to a ludicrous level of sin in an actual church. Make better sense to you now?

TRENT

Sure.

BART

You can take my land and fuck my wife; but never question my proficiency with the English language. I read your letter. At least I'm a better writer than you. Anyway, here's my question. (*BART stands.*) When we'd be fellowshipping at church, hanging out afterwards over coffee and donuts, being *friends*… did you want to take my wife away from me then? Were you studying? Learning how to take Terry from me?

TRENT

Theresa had her own reasons to be alienated.

BART

Oh excuse me. *Theresa.* Or were you just insinuating yourself into our graces to get on our land?

TRENT

None of this was planned, Bart. I know you don't believe me.

BART

Oh, no. I believe in you. I believe in monsters now, so I believe in you.

TRENT

The bag. Please.

BART throws the duffel at TRENT in a chest pass. Hard as he can. TRENT catches it.

TRENT

Thank you, Bart.

BART

Fuck you, Trent.

TRENT turns to go. BART calls after him, and he stops.

BART

I let you on this land. I'm the one who needs to be punished, I know that. You took my entire life away from me in a day. Why? I was a Christian to you. How can I end this?

Silently, EVAN watches BART from behind the screen door of the house.

TRENT

It is what it is, Bart. Things just happen.

BART

(Clumsily reaches in his pockets) Yes. Yes, things do happen. Trent. They happen all the time.

He pulls out a small-caliber handgun, and cradles it awkwardly in his hands.

TRENT

This isn't how it ends though. You don't want Theresa to remember you as a murderer.

The two men regard each other. Then TRENT turns and walks back to his car. BART stands and watches him go. As TRENT drives away, EVAN comes out of the house towards BART.

EVAN

Do you want Grandpa's watch? Bart. Billie says when we have the watch we have stories.

BART

(Walks unsteadily away from EVAN) Not now, Evan. Go back in the house.

EVAN

(Follows BART, holding out the watch) Billie says time. Time to wind the watch. Time.

BART

(Frustrated, flustered. He tries to push back at EVAN.) I said NO, Evan. Not now. Go away!

EVAN

Time, Bart. Billie says watch time. Time! Time! Time!

BART

BILLIE'S NOT HERE! SHE'S DEAD! SHE'S DEAD!

BART pushes EVAN back a few feet. He points the gun at EVAN.

BART

Stay away from me.

EVAN begins to rock and hum. BART suddenly realizes he's pointing a gun at his cousin. And then BART'S demeanor changes. He hums along with EVAN for a beat.

BART

I'm sorry, Evan. May I see the watch?

EVAN

Sure Bart. Time for watch.

EVAN hands the watch to BART, who gently tosses the watch a few feet forward into the yard. Just far enough to distract EVAN, who chases the sound where it falls. As BART turns and goes into the barn, EVAN cries.

EVAN

BILLIE! BILLIE MY WATCH NO NO NO NO BILLIE SAYS NO BILLIE SAYS NO NO NO NO…

EVAN'S cries bring ROB, CAM, JANE, and ADAIR out on the porch. They come down into the yard.

ADAIR

Evan? What happened? What's wrong?

EVAN

BILLIE SAYS WATCH TIME NO NO TIME NO TIME NO TIME

ADAIR

(Looking with EVAN) Wait… I found it. Evan, it's OK… here's Grandpa's watch. It's OK.

EVAN

(Calming) No time. Watch. Watch.

The sound of a gunshot comes from the barn. Everyone in the yard stops.

CAM

Bart.

ROB

Oh my God. BART!

ROB, CAM, and JANE run to the barn. A light turns on inside, followed by screams. ADAIR stays in the yard with EVAN, afraid to run into the barn.

EVAN cradles his head in his hands and rocks and self-soothes quietly for the rest of this scene.

EVAN

(Repeating) Time… time… time

ROB

(Within) BART! NO!

CAM

(Within) WAIT! ROB, WAIT! IS HE BREATHING? BART!

ROB

BART! BART!

JANE

(Running out of the barn) ADAIR! ADAIR! HE'S BREATHING! WHERE ARE THE KEYS TO THE TRUCK? WE NEED A PHONE!

JANE comes running out of the barn. Her hands are covered in blood.

JANE

We need to get him into town. We need a blanket to carry him, I need the keys to Cam's truck, they're on the mantel. My cell phone is next to the keys… *(JANE sees the blood on her hands)* I… I can't dial, there's too much… Oh my God in heaven there's so much blood THERE'S SO MUCH—

ADAIR grabs JANE'S shoulders.

ADAIR

Aunt Jane! Look at me! Look at me! I got it. I got it. Keys, blanket, cell phone. Is he okay? Tell me he's okay?

JANE

I don't know Adair… I just / don't know

ADAIR

Go. Get back in there. Take Highway 30 in, you hear me? I'll have the patrol meet you on the road! I'll stay here with Evan. Go! Take Highway 30!

ADAIR runs into the house as JANE runs back into the barn.
EVAN remains on the ground, cradling his watch.

EVAN

Time... time... time...

Lights down.

Memorial Day: Midnight

MAT sits on the porch steps beside EVAN. He holds the watch in his hands.

MAT

Let's see, what else can I tell you about my Dad? I don't have stories so much as I have specific memories, you know? Like how he took a magic marker and traced an outline of each tool on the pegboard of his workbench. So when you needed a hammer, there was this little crime scene outline displayed until you put the tool back where it belonged.

ADAIR listens from behind the screen door.

I was the youngest, so when my Mom left us I took it the worst. I didn't really understand. And Dad was working two jobs and caring for all of us—not a lot of space for quality time. So, I just followed him around, wherever he went. If my eyes were on him, he couldn't leave, you know? I would squeeze myself quietly into a corner and just, I don't know, keep my eye on him. I always wonder what he thought of that; having a tiny ghost in Tuffskins peering up at him from the darkness. He never acknowledged that he knew I was there. And then one day he was painting a model of an Indian motorcycle. His glasses were perched on the end of his nose, like Geppetto; so meticulous, so serene. I loved to watch him tinker. And he never even looked up when all of a sudden, he said, "Mateo. Come help me with this." And I actually

looked around the basement for Mateo until I realized that was
me. He wanted my help. And he scooted an apple crate next to
his stool so I could stand on it. I'm sure my eyes had to have been
enormous. And he said, "Hold this steady for me." And I did. I
still have that Indian motorcycle. *(He turns over the watch in his
hands)* He would have liked this watch a lot, Evan. He would have
appreciated how well you take care of it. *(Hands it to him)* Here
you go.

EVAN

Billie gave me this.

MAT

She sounds like she was a real special lady.

EVAN

She is.

ADAIR

(Coming out to the porch) Yes, she was.

MAT

Was that Jane you were talking to?

ADAIR

Yes. She's staying with Bart tonight. Uncle Cam and Dad are on
their way back here.

MAT

I eavesdropped a bit. Did I hear that he's conscious?

ADAIR

He was, for a bit. The doctor says he'll be in and out of it for a few
days. But they're pretty confident that it's just a skull fracture.

MAT

Wow. That's...

ADAIR

Lucky. I know.

MAT

That's one word for it.

ADAIR

There are so many horrible images going through my mind right now. I can't make them stop. I can't stop thinking "what if?"

MAT

In all probability, you would be saying "if only" right now.

ADAIR

(Nods) Thank you for being here. You didn't have to come out.

MAT

I wanted to be here.

ADAIR

Do you still talk to your mom?

MAT

She tried to re-engage when I was starting college. I never know what to say to her. I don't try very hard.

ADAIR

Sounds like she's trying. You should try too.

MAT

Why?

ADAIR

Because she's your mom. There are so many things I never learned from Mom while she was still here. How to make pie dough from scratch, how to mend things... I used to sit with her in this spot. When I was in college, she'd let me bum a cigarette and we'd solve the world's problems. I think about the advice she gave me on all these petty, tiny things I thought were such tragedies. But stuff like tonight... I could really use her advice right now.

MAT

I'm sorry.

ADAIR

I still talk to her. I hope that she's listening.

MAT

I'll bet she is. I believe that.

ADAIR

(Nodding) Yeah.

MAT

I'm heading up to Lincoln on Tuesday.

ADAIR

I know. I think I may need to stay here.

MAT

I know that. That wasn't going to be my question.

ADAIR

Oh. What was it?

MAT

What are you doing on Wednesday? *(Looks in the distance)* Car's coming.

ADAIR

(Nods) Dad and Uncle Cam.

MAT

I think I'll head inside with Evan while you talk to him. Would you mind?

ADAIR

Yes.

MAT

You would? You need me to stay here?

ADAIR

No. Yes to Wednesday.

MAT

(*Smiles, gathers his things*) Hey Evan, how about you and I head into the house? (*To ADAIR*) Okay by you?

ADAIR

Yes. Thank you, Mateo.

> *EVAN and MAT go into the house. Headlights shine across the yard, as CAM drops ROB off. ADAIR gives a wave. Sound of CAM's car receding… ROB comes into the yard. ADAIR jumps up and meets him halfway.*

ROB

Did you talk to Jane?

ADAIR

Yes. I just got off the phone with her.

ROB

How is he?

ADAIR

He's resting. He's stable.

ROB

They're bringing in a neurologist in the morning to make sure all's OK. Jesus… (*ROB gets a little unsteady. He sits*)

ADAIR

Dad, you OK?

ROB

I'm fine. I'm fine. I think the adrenaline's wearing off. Have you heard anything from Jane?

ADAIR

She just called. He's okay.

ROB

I could use a drink…

MAT has appeared on the porch, holding a bottle of whisky and two glasses. He smiles, nods, and leaves them on the porch.

MAT

Thought you might want this. You doing OK?

ROB

I am. Thank you, Mat. *(MAT exits to house)*

ADAIR

I'll hook you up. *(Goes to get the glasses, bottle)*

ROB

He's a nice boy.

ADAIR

(Pouring) Yes, he is. Good lawyer, too.

ROB

(Drinks) Did you talk to Jane?

ADAIR

Yes.

ROB

How is he?

ADAIR

He's resting, Dad. We'll head in first thing tomorrow.

ROB

(*Takes another drink*) Everything's a fog. There are these pictures flashing through my head. The hospital, the barn… But they're all jumbled together, out of sequence. I remember person after person after person telling me I'm lucky. That Bart's lucky…

ADAIR

I have a lot of those flashes too.

ROB

But… there are some things… (*He trails off*)

ADAIR

What things?

ROB

Things I don't think I know.

ADAIR

What?

ROB

(*Terrified whisper*) I don't know what I *don't* remember.

ADAIR

I don't understand.

ROB

What are the things that happened today that I don't remember? What did I say today that made him do this? What did I not remember to say to him that could have kept him / from…

ADAIR

Dad. Listen to me. This was not your fault.

ROB

I remember what he said!

ADAIR

We all said a lot of things. Things we shouldn't have said, but things you can forgive. Listen to me. They're all things you can forgive.

ROB

I can't remember your mother. I can't remember her eyes. I only remember the end, I can't remember the beginning, the—

ADAIR

I can help you remember.

ROB

I can't remember her last words to me!

ADAIR

They were that she loved you.

ROB

(His eyes widen in horror) St. Kilda… I remember St. Kilda! Oh God, I remember St. Kilda. The dogs…

ADAIR

Who is St. Kilda?

ROB

The dogs! The compromise! The villagers could leave, but no animal could remain, so they all led their dogs down to the pier, tied stones around their necks, and threw them into the ocean.

ADAIR

Dad, what are you talking about?

ROB

(Hands over his eyes, he keens) The dogs! I can't stop seeing the dogs! They drowned all their dogs in the ocean! They were so trusting, so loyal! Oh God, what have I done?

ADAIR

I don't understand. Please, Dad, tell me what you mean.

ROB

(Seizes ADAIR by the shoulders) Listen to me! When the villagers evacuated, there were still some small children with them.

ADAIR

You're scaring me.

ROB

The children *thrived.* They moved away from there and they were fine!

ADAIR

And we will be fine. Bart will be fine—

ROB

None of this is worth it without both of you. I would burn this place to the ground if I knew it would keep you safe...

ADAIR

I know, Dad. I know. *(She rocks him gently)* I know... I know...

Lights down.

Labor Day

Mid-afternoon. CAM and BART are replacing a support beam underneath the porch. The radio is turned on to the football game, and they listen while they work. There is a cooler of beer on the picnic table. ADAIR storms in from around the barn.

ADAIR

Dad! Where's Dad? *(Points to the feet sticking out under the porch)* Is that Dad? Dad?

CAM

No, that's Bart. Your Dad's in the house. What's wrong?

ADAIR

(At foot of stairs) DAD? HEY, DAD!?!

BART

(Out from under the porch. He wears a feed cap) You could just walk in the house.

ADAIR

DAD!!!!

> *ROB comes out on the porch.*

ROB

What?

ADAIR

I just heard that you hired on Virgil and Ray McNeff, is that true?

ROB

It's harvest time.

ADAIR

Were you planning on sharing that information with me anytime soon?

ROB

I just talked to Ray yesterday.

ADAIR

So *now* you hire them on? I told you I was going to help out.

ROB

I'm planning on that.

ADAIR

So you don't think I'm able to help.

ROB

I never said that. You're going to court next week!

ADAIR

I'm well prepared, and I can do both! I can't believe you still think I can't pull my own weight around here!

ROB

I never said you couldn't!

> *ADAIR stalks over to the tool box, starts sifting through the tools for wire cutters.*

ADAIR

I can do all the things that Ray and Virgil do. I did them all before I moved away, and I know I can do them better. *(Points wire cutters at BART)* How hard have I been working to get ready for harvest?

BART

Yikes. Really hard?

ADAIR

Really hard!

ROB

I just thought you might want to spend more time working on the case.

ADAIR

(Whirls) What? You think I'm not?

ROB

(Holds up his hands) Whoa-Whoa-Whoa!

ADAIR

Do you know how many hours I've spent preparing? Do you realize how much you need to prepare, bringing a case before the Supreme Court? To memorize all the statistics? The case law? I have to anticipate hundreds of possible questions from the judges, and be ready with a succinct response for every single one. In 2005, a group of greedy dimwits in New London, Connecticut tore down a bunch of people's homes to make way for a shopping center that never even got *built*, and the US Supreme Court agreed for some jack-hole reason that was A-okay. That's eminent domain for private profit. And now we're all paying for that jack-hole case out here! Since 1986, there have been at least 7,978 pipeline incidents; injuring or killing 2,872 Americans at a cost of almost 7 trillion dollars! So yes, I'm ready, okay? I am extraordinarily prepared, and I can bring in the harvest better than Virgil and Ray. Don't ever doubt my capabilities!

  Beat.

CAM

All right.

ROB

Are you always like this before you try a case?

ADAIR

Probably.

ROB

Makes you fun to be around.

ADAIR

What I *don't* need / is you

ROB

(Holds out his hands) Hold up, Atticus! They're coming on temporarily! Bart's heading out soon, and I want to make sure we're covered. I want to make sure you're not all stressed out—

ADAIR

I am not stressed out!

ROB

You wanna loosen your grip on those wire cutters? You're white-knuckling that thing! *(ADAIR looks at her hand)* I know you can do all this. Bart's been bragging about you.

ADAIR

Yeah?

BART

Yeah. You got this.

ADAIR

It's just important.

ROB

I know.

ADAIR

Okay. Well, I'm going to go finish up at the henhouse. I'm heading into town tonight.

CAM

You going to see Mat?

ADAIR

We've tons of prep work to get done before next week.

BART

But I thought you just said you were "extraordinarily prepared."

Beat. ADAIR'S stumped. She tries not to appear bashful.

BART

(Throws his hands up) Please tell me you're going to be better than this in court.

ADAIR

Shut up.

It is now open teasing season on ADAIR.

BART

(Grins) You shut up.

CAM

You are looking extraordinarily blushy there, sister.

ROB

You *are* blushy! By the ears! You see it right there?

ADAIR

Knock it off.

THE BOYS

(Falsetto) OOOOOOOOOOOOOH...

ADAIR

(Arms akimbo) Stop it!

THE BOYS

(Mimicking her back) STOP IT!

Roars from the boys. ADAIR notices a car approaching.

ADAIR

Bart, how about you give me a hand at the henhouse?

BART

It's chicken wire, Adair, Jesus. You don't have to be an architect—

Sound of gravel in the drive. All turn to see that it's JANE.
There's a tense beat as everyone looks at BART.

BART

She and I gotta sort this out before I leave. Might as well be now.

JANE enters the yard. She smiles and is friendly, but there is a
distinctive chill towards BART.

CAM

Hey there! You been listening to the game?

JANE

Not after the third turnover! We're just terrible this year.

BART

Still got another half to go!

JANE

Where's Evan? Thought I'd take him into town with me.

BART

He's out at the coop. Want me to go get him?

JANE

Cam, would you mind getting him? I know he'll come quick if
you go.

BART

(*Smiles. Keeps trying*) Nah, I can do it. I'll get him back here for
you.

JANE

Cam? Could you please? I prefer you do it.

BART

Hang on. I'm going to try an experiment here. *(He walks into JANE'S eyeline.)* Hey. Can you say my name out loud?

JANE

… Cam?

BART

Oh, come on, Aunt Jane! You can't stay mad at me. How many times do you need me to say it? I'm sorry. I was stupid, and I was drunk. Why are you still punishing me? I'd really like to make this right with you before I go. I love you. *(Tries to joke)* I mean, I need to have another member of my family mad at me like I need another hole in the head—

JANE swings back and slaps BART across the face. Hard. Then again.

JANE

Don't you ever joke about that with me. Don't you make any jokes like that, *ever*. I am so mad at you, Bartholomew MacLeod. I have all this anger, and I have no place to set it down! Do you know what you did when you shot yourself that night? You turned your back on your family. You turned your back on me. You may have been drunk, but you weren't stupid. You had a house full of the people who love you the most, fifty feet from where you stood. We were there to help you bear the weight of that day! No one should ever witness what I saw when I ran into the barn that night. It tore everything that was human right out of me. I hated God in that moment; I even hated you. *(She looks at him)* You will always have the most beautiful smile I have ever seen, and you walk this earth with such a happy grace. The day you learned to walk, you toddled right up to me and called me by my name; and I knew then that I would love you more fiercely than you could ever know. And now, when I see you, I am reminded of how close I was to losing you, and that terrible night happens to me all over again. (*She seizes him by the shoulders*) I love you. I will work my way over this. Every one of us is guaranteed equal shares of devastation in this life. Loss. All we're asked to do is fight our way through. I need you to do that, Bart. I need to believe you're going to be all right. (*JANE holds him tightly, quickly, then lets him go.*) I'll be in the car. (*Exits*)

> BART *watches her go. He turns to see ROB, ADAIR, and CAM looking at him.*

ROB

(*Indicates in JANE'S direction with his wrench*) What she said.

BART

I didn't know that's how she felt.

CAM

Sometimes it takes her a little time to figure it out herself. (*Notices EVAN coming around the house with a bucket of eggs.*) Evan, you got a lot of eggs there.

EVAN

There are 14 eggs.

ROB

We'll have ourselves some omelets later maybe. I'll take these in for you, buddy.

CAM

Your mom's in the car—want to go into town?

EVAN

Yes.

CAM

(*Polishes off his beer*) Rob, we just need to tighten those carriage bolts at each end, and we're good to go.

ROB

Sounds good.

CAM

(Claps BART on the shoulder as he goes) See you later!

BART

See you. *(Beat. BART stands awkwardly for a moment.)*

ROB

Hey. Can I get a hand over here?

BART AND ADAIR

You bet.

    ROB and BART work on the car while ADAIR pulls out a beer.

ROB

So, how's the packing coming?

BART

Pretty much done. Just need to pull together the books I want to take.

ROB

I think they still have books in California.

BART

They just don't have mine.

ROB

Can't remember a time when you didn't have a book on the dashboard, or had a paperback sticking out of your back pocket.

ADAIR

Oh! There's this beautiful hidden spot on the campus right next to a brook. It's great for reading and writing, and super close to my place. I'll map it for you.

BART

Thanks.

ADAIR

Sorry I blew up about Virgil and Ray.

ROB

Yeah. I figure we'll be good as long as Virgil doesn't leave his teeth lying around everywhere.

ADAIR

Remember when he left his teeth on the dinner table?

BART

(Chuckles) That was so nasty.. Terry was clearing the dishes and she had them in her hand before she realized what she was holding. God, the screams. (Small beat)

ROB

Adair, hand me that spatula, will you?

ADAIR

The what?

ROB

The spatula. (Points) Right there.

ADAIR

What?

ROB

It's right in front of you.

ADAIR

(Laughing) You need a *spatula*?

ROB

Yes!

ADAIR

What do you need a spatula *for?*

ROB

(Snaps) Don't be smart with me! Give me the spatula!

ADAIR and BART look at ROB.

ROB

(Points) That spatula! What's the matter with you? *(Irritated)* Jesus Christ, may I have the spatula please?

BART

(Holds up a wrench) This spatula right here?

ROB

Yes, that spatula right there! For God's sake! *(BART hands him the wrench, and ROB continues his work as he talks.)* Listen, I had my doubts about this whole switcheroo you kids agreed to, but at least having the two of you separated will give me a little relief from you both giving me guff all the time; the minute you're both in the same room you still behave like 10-year-old monkeys. I've only got so much patience! You got it?

ADAIR

(Looking at BART) I got it.

BART acknowledges ADAIR with a nod as ROB continues to clean up tools.

ROB

All right then. *(Slams the tool box closed)* California. I always lose you kids to California.

Beat.

BART

You can always come visit.

ROB

(*A bit grumpy*) Hmmph.

ADAIR

Was that a no?

BART

I think that was a hell no. Are you pouting?

ROB

I don't pout. There's no need for me to go to California.

BART

Oh, I get it. It's a communist state. Afraid you might be
brainwashed? *Comrade?*

ROB

That's ridiculous.

ADAIR

(*Chuckling*) You never know… look what happened to me!

ROB

Yeah, look what happened to you.

   ADAIR laughs.

BART

She always did have 'granola' tendencies. It was inevitable.

ADAIR

(*Laughing*) That's right, you never know. You could walk off the
plane, order a salad, and boom. You fall in love with quinoa.
That's how it starts.

ROB

Quinoa? Who's that? Is she your landlord?

   BART and ADAIR roar with laughter.

BART

No, no… it's something that you eat. It's a grain.

ADAIR

It's very healthy.

ROB

Like a soybean?

ADAIR

More like a lentil.

BART

A lentil with tiny little legs.

They all laugh.

ROB

Holy hell. I don't need my salad walking to me. No, you just come back here, all right?

BART

All right.

ROB

(Feeling the word out) Quinoa… huh. Sounds like something those Tibetan monks would chant in the National Geographic. *(He chants like a Tibetan monk)* Quinoa….quinoa….

ADAIR and BART laugh, and then begin to chant along with ROB, smiling.

ADAIR AND BART

Quinoa… Quinoa… Quinoa…

They chant as the sun sets over the porch, their chant possibly moving into a harmony as the lights fade.

Samhain

Late afternoon. The MacLeod farmstead reflects the end of the harvest. The flowers have been cleared from the window boxes, there is a chill in the air. ADAIR walks out of the house towards the fields, pulling on her work gloves. She wears a Carhartt coat and irrigation boots. When she's halfway across the yard, ROB comes out on the porch and hollers to her.

ROB

Adair, hold up a minute!

ADAIR

Yeah?

ROB

Are you heading out to the East pasture?

ADAIR

Heading out to the elevator.

ROB

Virgil just rang me. He says we've got a fence down over by the white gate.

CAM and EVAN round the corner of the barn.

ADAIR

Ugh. It's about to rain!

ROB

Lemme grab my boots and we'll get ahead of the jailbreak.

CAM

What's up?

ADAIR

Fence down.

CAM

Ughhhh…

ADAIR

Right?

CAM

Rob, you want me to go?

ROB

Nah, I just need to get supper off the burner and I'll be right out. *(Turns to exit)*

ADAIR

Hang on!

ROB

What?

ADAIR

Could you repeat that?

ROB

What? Supper?

ADAIR

It's just that you sound so domestic and sassy.

CAM

You do keep a very pretty kitchen these days, Julia. Looking forward to reading them hints you send to Heloise.

EVAN is approaching the stairs with his watch to sit down in front of ROB.

ROB

Hilarious. That's right Evan, protect these harpies from my vengeful wrath. *(Looking up the road)* Well Adair, your worm has turned, chickadee-dee-dee. Your boyfriend's coming up the road.

ADAIR

(Looking) Stop calling him my boyfriend.

CAM

Then what were you two doing behind the barn the other day? Red Cross training?

ADAIR

Jesus Christ.

CAM

Happiest heart attack I've ever seen!

ROB

(Roars with mock outrage) THAT BRUTE! Taking my teenaged daughter back behind the barn?!? He's besmirched your honor! I'll have his manhood! Wait a minute. You're not a teenager.

ADAIR

No.

ROB

NEVERTHELESS! Cam? Can I refer to her as "aged? *('age-ed')*" Can I say he "besmirched my aged daughter?"

ADAIR

I am standing right here! Objectified like a piece of meat!

ROB

I didn't objectify you! He did, behind the barn!

MAT somberly enters the yard.

ROB

(*To Mat, more mock outrage*) A-HA! MASHER, J'ACCUSE!
BESMIRCHER OF DAUGHTERS, DEFEND YOURSELF!!

ADAIR

(*Turning to Mat*) Mat, they're acting like church ladies, don't…
(*She stops*) What is it?

MAT

We lost. I just got the call.

> *Beat.*

ADAIR

No.

CAM

We lost?

ROB

What?

ADAIR

No, no / no

MAT

The case. Rob, we lost the case.

ADAIR

Oh my God, NO!

MAT

Adair, I'm so sorry. I really thought we had a chance.

ADAIR

We had more than a chance! This makes no sense!

CAM

Tell me what this means.

MAT

It means they can move forward.

ROB

Tomorrow?

ADAIR

Jesus Christ.

ROB

Mat, could they be here tomorrow?

CAM

Can you take it to a higher court?

ADAIR

No.

MAT

You don't know that.

ADAIR

Of course I know that! So do you! Our chance to stop it was *right here*, in this state! We gathered all the data; we gave them all the facts! What did I do? What did I miss?

MAT

(Approaching ADAIR) You didn't miss anything, Adair. We'll find another—

ADAIR

(Slaps MAT'S hand away angrily) Don't touch me! You don't understand! I waded in that spring over that hill when I was a child! I drank cold water from that pump over there every summer! I picked that strawberry field every July with my mother. The aquifer has always been here under our feet. This pipeline *will* break. If it happens over the aquifer there's no sucking the poison out. *That is the truth,* but nobody wants to listen. Everybody just wants to fight. Nobody is *listening,* Nobody / is listening!

ROB

Hey! Adair! Adair! Look at me!

ADAIR

This is my *home!*

ROB

Adair MacLeod! Look at me!

ADAIR stops. She's devastated.

ADAIR

I can't... I'm sorry, I can't.

ROB

Eyes here, Adair. *(ADAIR meets ROB'S eye)* Don't push him away. Don't push any of us away. You did your job, and you did the best you could.

ADAIR

Everything's turned upside down.

ROB

Well, then don't lie down and let the sky fall on you. You take all this weight on yourself, you'll never get back up. You understand what I'm saying to you?

ADAIR

No. I'm / sorry—

ROB

Look down at where you're standing. Right there, between your toes. *(He slaps the porch railing)* This house was built on the foundations of my dad's four-room shack, which was built over a sod house your great-great-grandfather burrowed out of the earth. And before we were here, somebody else was here. And fought. I've been thinking about that a lot. This land taught me who I am. I understand a lot better why the folk that came before me fought. It's the land that makes us better, Adair. It's the land that's sheltered and provided for us and our babies, and will for whoever comes after us. Our job is to make sure whoever gets it next does right by it. You know what that means?

ADAIR

I'm not sure.

ROB

Anybody who's walked their farm from dark of morning to dark of night knows you never, *ever*, walk away from the land that needs you and feeds you. Look at all the stuff this country throws at us: twisters, drought, fire, floods, dust, death? You are a child of this land, Adair. You're a child of mine too so I figure you already have some ideas sparking up in that brain of yours.

ADAIR

(Wiping her eyes) Yeah, a few.

ROB

Well then, we got a fence to mend before the rain comes. You ready?

ADAIR

Yeah.

MAT

Can I help?

ADAIR

I'd like that.

ROB

You want to set him up with some rain-gear?

ADAIR

Sure thing. *(She and Mat head for the house)*

ROB

(*Calling after them*) There's nothing better for strategic thinking than fixing a barbed wire fence!

ROB sits wearily on the steps next to EVAN. CAM joins them.

CAM

I'll lend a hand out there too, Rob. You stay here.

ROB

Okay.

CAM

You all right?

ROB

Yeah.

CAM

I wish there were…

ROB

Hey. (*Beat*) Appreciate it.

CAM

I'm sorry, Rob.

ROB

Wish I could blame you.

CAM

That was good stuff you said back there.

ROB

Did you buy it?

CAM

You did good.

ROB

Well.

CAM

Yeah. *(He reaches over and gives EVAN a ruffle. EVAN lets him take the watch from him.)* Thanks Evan. Yeah, we do okay. What you said about the land? I think God does have a little hand in all this too.

ROB snorts.

CAM

I know, I know. I'm consorting with the enemy. Lemme tell you though, I've never told anybody this story—not even Jane. Evan wasn't even two years old. He was still rambunctious, engaged. He looked us in the eye; still called us by our names. He had his own world then too, I realize. He was playing some pretend game, ripping around the living room before bedtime. Burning down the energy from the day. I was across the room in my easy chair, and I watched him approach the stairs and look up. I wasn't worried, he never went up there. But all of a sudden, he charged right on up without stopping. And before I could get up there to chase him, I watched him lose his balance on the very top step and pitch backwards. I was too far away to stop him from tumbling backwards down all those steps. *(He considers)* You know, there's that moment you realize something terrible is about to happen, where time just slows down? That moment every cell in your body becomes a desperate prayer. Evan seemed to hang forever up there, his hands out—this eternity before the fall. Then all at once I saw his entire body shift right back up. Into balance. It was as if somebody's hand just came down around the back of his head, and *ootched* him back up. And then he leaned down, climbed up the last stair onto the carpet, and on he went down the upstairs hallway.

So maybe it's not God doing the work. But what if there's someone else watching over us, doing the work for Him. That little *ootch* every once in a while to keep us safe. I look for those moments every day.

ROB

Yeah.

CAM

Well, that one word out of you is enough to put in my win column for the day. *(A lazy flash of lightning as ADAIR and MAT come out of the house)* All right! I'll head out there with you. *(CAM hands the watch to ROB as he exits)* Late in the year for thunder. Strange weather this whole year. Be back soon!

ADAIR

You okay here?

ROB

Yep! Gonna hang with Evan here and get supper back on the range. *(ADAIR walks ahead with CAM)* Mat, you got her?

MAT

I got her.

ROB

I'll set a plate for you.

> ADAIR and MAT exit.

ROB

(Calling after them) We got pirate plots to scheme after you batten down the hatches! *(Low thunder rumbles in the distance. ROB and EVAN are alone on the porch. ROB turns the watch in his hands.)* Evan, your Aunt Billie sure knew what she was doing when she gave you my dad's watch. My father was a good, good man, but he didn't talk much. Made it hard to know if I was doing the right thing sometimes. I will always associate this watch with him, sitting with him in the silence, turning this over and over in my hands.

EVAN

Watch. Billie says watch.

ROB

Yeah... she sure did a good job of keeping everybody safe around
here. Making everybody feel loved. I sure wish I could tell her
how we're doing. That I worry at night. That sometimes I get so
tired. I do get awful tired.

EVAN

Billie says watch.

ROB

I wish I could tell her I miss her.

EVAN'S voice suddenly changes; an eminent power beneath it.

EVAN

Billie says watch.

*ROB turns to look at EVAN, who is looking out across the
fields. Suddenly, a flash of lightning or sunbeam of light shines
brilliantly down upon his face, making him appear as if he is
almost lit from within. ROB turns out to look in the distance,
stunned. Could it be?*

Then he smiles. A long, low rumble of thunder comes in reply.

ROB

I love you too.

Lights fade to blackout.

~ *End of play* ~

ABOUT THE AUTHOR

LAURA LEININGER-CAMPBELL is an actor, playwright and photographer. She received her theater training from Connecticut College, the National Theater Institute, and received the Lee Strasberg Institute Scholarship, training in New York City. As a playwright, Laura has written a number of adaptations for Joslyn Castle's Literary Festival, including Bram Stoker's *The Jewel of Seven Stars* and *Dangerous Beauty,* a retelling of Oscar Wilde's novel *The Picture of Dorian Gray.* Her original script, *Eminent Domain,* was a 2016 Eugene O'Neill National Playwrights Conference finalist and had its world premiere at the Omaha Community Playhouse in August 2017.

www.lalaplaywright.com

www.ingramcontent.com/pod-product-compliance
Lightning Source LLC
LaVergne TN
LVHW051737080426
835511LV00018B/3119